THE VAGUS NERVE UNLOCKING THE BODY'S SUPERHIGHWAY

A Journey into Healing, Wellness, and Mind-Body Harmony

MONIKA DANIEL

© Copyright 2024 - All rights reserved. The contents of this book may not be reproduced, duplicated or transmitted without direct written permission from the author. Under no circumstances will any legal responsibility or blame be held against the publisher for any reparation, damages, or monetary loss due to the information herein, either directly or indirectly.

Legal Notice: This book is copyright protected. This is only for personal use. You cannot amend, distribute, sell, use, quote or paraphrase any part or the content within this book without the consent of the author.

Disclaimer Notice: Please note the information contained within this document is for educational and entertainment purposes only. Every attempt has been made to provide accurate, up to date and reliable complete information. No warranties of any kind are expressed or implied. Readers acknowledge that the author is not engaging in the rendering of legal, financial, medical or professional advice. The content of this book has been derived from various sources. Please consult a licensed professional before attempting any techniques outlined in this book. By reading this document, the reader agrees that under no circumstances is the author responsible for any losses, direct or indirect, which are incurred as a result of the use of information contained within this document, including, but not limited to, errors, omissions, or inaccuracies.

Table of Contents

Chapter 1: Introduction to the Vagus Nerve 1

    An Overview of the Nervous System 2
    The Discovery and Significance of the Vagus Nerve 4
    How to Harness the Power of the Vagus Nerve 7

Chapter 2: Anatomy and Functions of the Vagus Nerve 9

    Primary Functions in the Body 12
    What is Vagal Tone? 15
    The Benefits of Working With the Vagus Nerve 15
    When the Vagus Nerve Isn't Functioning Well 17
    What is the State of Your Vagus Nerve? 19

Chapter 3: The Vagus Nerve and the Autonomic Nervous System 23

    The Role of the Vagus Nerve in the Parasympathetic System 25
    Achieving Balance Between the Sympathetic and Parasympathetic Systems 27

Chapter 4: The Vagus Nerve and Mental Health 31

    Influence on Mood and Emotional Regulation 31
    Connection to Anxiety, Depression, and Stress 34
    How to Use the Vagus Nerve to Improve
    Mental Health 36

Chapter 5: The Vagus Nerve and Physical Health 43

    Impact on Cardiovascular Health 44
    Role in Digestion and Gut Health 46
    Effects on Immune Response and Inflammation 49
    Vagus Nerve Strategies to Improve Physical Health 52

Chapter 6: The Vagus Nerve and Chronic Illness 57

    Connection to Chronic Pain and Fibromyalgia 58
    The Vagus Nerve's Role in Autoimmune Diseases 60
    Vagal Nerve Stimulation as a Treatment Option 63

Chapter 7: Vagus Nerve Stimulation Techniques 69

    Overview of Vagus Nerve Stimulation (VNS) 69
    Non-invasive Techniques to Stimulate the `
    Vagus Nerve 72
    Medical Devices and Surgical Options 84

Table of Contents

Chapter 8: The Mind-Body Connection 89

   How the Vagus Nerve Mediates the Mind-Body Connection 91

   Practice to Enhance Vagal Tone 93

   The Importance of Emotional and Psychological Health 110

Chapter 9: Diet, Nutrition, and the Vagus Nerve 115

   The Impact of Diet on Vagal Tone 116

   Good vs. Bad Eating Habits 120

   How Crash Diets and Binge Eating Affect the Vagus Nerve 123

Chapter 10: Lifestyle Changes for Vagus Nerve Health ... 127

   Stress Management Techniques 128

   The Importance of Sleep and Relaxation 144

   Exercise and its Effects on the Vagus Nerve 147

Chapter 11: Case Studies and Personal Stories 151

Chapter 12: Future Directions and Conclusion 157

Resources for Further Learning 163

Conclusion 167

References 171

About the Author

Monika Daniel, the founder of www.reikisoulacademy.com, is not just a passionate Reiki Master but also a mother of two daughters. This role has significantly influenced her practice, bringing a wealth of compassion and empathy to her work. Her understanding of the importance of nurturing and caring for oneself and others has been deepened through her motherhood journey and her dedication to holistic healing.

Monika's personal journey into the holistic side of life began in Kho Phangyang, Thailand. This journey, filled with self-discovery and growth, led her to embrace a wide array of healing modalities, with a particular focus on Reiki and energy work. Her studies and experiences have enriched her understanding of the healing potential that lies within each of us, inspiring her to share these transformative practices with others.

Monika's commitment to promoting health and wellness is not just a part of her life, it is her life. She is deeply passionate about healthy living, nutrition, and mindfulness, and she actively incorporates these principles into her daily life and teachings, inspiring others to do the same.

Monika's commitment to holistic healing extends beyond her individual practice. She is not just an organizer of retreats; she is a leader. Her passion and dedication create nurturing spaces for individuals to reconnect with themselves and experience profound healing and transformation. Her leadership in these retreats provides a sanctuary for participants to explore holistic practices, cultivate self-awareness, and embark on personal growth and empowerment journeys, instilling a sense of trust and confidence in her abilities.

With a warm heart and an unwavering commitment to the well-being of others, Monika Daniel continues to inspire and uplift those on their path to health, healing, and holistic living.

She dedicates this book to her darling daughters, Sophia and Holly, and her husband, who has supported her throughout this transformative journey.

Chapter 1

Introduction to the Vagus Nerve

Welcome to the fascinating world of the vagus nerve, the unsung hero of our nervous system. In this chapter, we're going to delve deep into the intricate workings of this remarkable nerve, shedding light on its crucial role in regulating various bodily functions and influencing our overall health and well-being.

The vagus nerve, also known as the "wandering nerve," is like the ultimate multitasker, overseeing a wide range of functions such as heart rate, digestion, and even mood. It's basically the behind-the-scenes superstar keeping everything in check without asking for much recognition.

As we journey through the complexities of the vagus nerve, you'll discover how it acts as a powerful communication pathway between the brain and the body, playing a key role in the intricate dance of signals that keep us in balance. From its impact on our stress response to its connection to inflammation and immune function, the vagus nerve truly embodies the saying, "mind over matter."

An Overview of the Nervous System

Before we can really explore the vagus nerve and its uses, we need to go a little deeper. That means we need to explore the nervous system in more detail.

The nervous system is a fascinating and intricate network that serves as the command center of the human body. It is responsible for controlling everything from basic reflexes to complex cognitive functions. Let's take a closer look at this amazing system that allows us to move, think, feel, and experience the world around us.

At the core of the nervous system is the brain, which acts as the control center. It processes information received from the body's sensory organs and sends out signals to direct the body's responses. The brain is divided into different regions, each responsible for specific functions such as motor control, language processing, memory, and emotions.

Connected to the brain is the spinal cord, which runs down the length of the back and serves as a communication highway between the brain and the rest of the body. The spinal cord is responsible for transmitting sensory information from the body to the brain and carrying motor signals from the brain to the muscles.

The nervous system is divided into two main parts: the central nervous system (CNS) and the peripheral nervous system (PNS). The CNS consists of the brain and spinal cord, while the PNS includes all the nerves that branch out from the CNS to reach every part of the body.

Within the PNS, there are two subdivisions: the somatic nervous system and the autonomic nervous system. The somatic nervous system is responsible for voluntary movements and sensory information, while the autonomic nervous system controls involuntary processes such as heart rate, digestion, and breathing.

One of the key components of the nervous system is the neuron, which is a specialized cell that transmits electrical and chemical signals. Neurons communicate with each other through a structure called a synapse, where neurotransmitters are released to carry signals across the small gap between neurons.

The nervous system also includes supporting cells called glial cells, which provide structural support for neurons, insulate them, and help with their nutrition. Glial cells play a crucial role in maintaining the overall health and function of the nervous system.

In addition to neurons and glial cells, the nervous system also includes specialized cells called sensory receptors, which detect various stimuli such as light, sound, touch, and temperature. These receptors convert sensory input into electrical signals that can be processed by the brain.

The nervous system is constantly receiving and processing information from the environment to help us respond to changes and maintain homeostasis. It coordinates voluntary movements, regulates essential bodily functions, and enables us to experience sensations and emotions.

It's truly amazing to think about how the nervous system works seamlessly to keep us alive and functioning every day. From the simplest reflex actions to the most complex thoughts and behaviors, the nervous system is at the heart of everything we do.

The vagus nerve plays a crucial role in our complex nervous system. As the longest cranial nerve, it meanders its way from the brainstem through the neck and thorax, all the way down to the abdomen, forming a vital bridge of communication between the brain and various organs.

The Discovery and Significance of the Vagus Nerve

The vagus nerve was first discovered by a talented anatomist named Francis Glisson in the 17th century. Glisson's curiosity led him to uncover what would later be recognized as one of the most significant nerves in the body.

Introduction to the Vagus Nerve

The vagus nerve, also known as the 10th cranial nerve, is a long and wandering nerve that starts at the base of the brain and branches out like a complex network, reaching various parts of the body, including the heart, lungs, stomach, and intestines. Its name "vagus" is derived from the Latin word meaning "wandering," aptly describing its meandering path throughout the body.

The significance of the vagus nerve lies in its role as the primary component of the parasympathetic nervous system, the part of the autonomic nervous system responsible for regulating rest and digest functions. This nerve acts as a superhighway for communication between the brain and the body, relaying crucial information and controlling essential bodily functions.

One of the most remarkable features of the vagus nerve is its bidirectional communication system. Not only does it transmit signals from the brain to the body, but it also sends feedback from the body to the brain. This constant dialogue between the two ensures that our bodily functions are finely tuned and regulated, maintaining a delicate balance necessary for our overall well-being.

Research into the vagus nerve has revealed its profound impact on various aspects of human health. Studies have shown that stimulating the vagus nerve can have therapeutic effects on conditions such as epilepsy, depression, and even inflammatory disorders. This has led to the development of innovative treatments such as vagus nerve stimulation therapy, which holds promise for improving the lives of many individuals suffering from these conditions.

Furthermore, the vagus nerve plays a crucial role in the body's stress response system. When activated, it helps to modulate the body's fight-or-flight response, promoting a sense of calm and relaxation. This is why activities such as deep breathing, meditation, and yoga, which stimulate the vagus nerve, are often recommended for stress relief and overall well-being.

The vagus nerve's influence extends beyond physical health and into the realm of emotional well-being. It is often referred to as the "wanderer of emotions," as it is intricately linked to our feelings and mood regulation. By understanding the connection between the vagus nerve and emotional health, we can explore new avenues for promoting mental wellness and resilience.

In addition to its role in health and well-being, the vagus nerve also holds intriguing implications for the field of neuroscience. Scientists continue to unravel the mysteries of this complex nerve, seeking to understand its intricate pathways and how they influence our thoughts, behaviors, and perceptions. The vagus nerve serves as a gateway to unlocking the secrets of the mind-body connection, bridging the gap between our physical and emotional experiences.

How to Harness the Power of the Vagus Nerve

Exploring the wonders of the vagus nerve is like peeking into the intricate machinery that powers our body and mind. This mighty nerve serves as the communication highway between your brain and various organs, impacting everything from digestion to mood. By delving deeper into the world of the vagus nerve, you can unlock a treasure trove of knowledge that may potentially revolutionize your understanding of health and well-being.

Learning more about the vagus nerve can be likened to embarking on a thrilling journey of self-discovery. It's like uncovering a hidden superpower within yourself—one that holds the key to regulating stress, improving digestion, enhancing your immune system, and even fostering a greater sense of calm and relaxation.

In essence, understanding the vagus nerve can provide you with a deeper appreciation of the remarkable interconnectedness of your body and mind. So, why not take a step further into this fascinating realm and empower yourself with valuable insights that could truly enrich your life? The vagus nerve beckons, inviting you to discover its secrets and embrace the potential for greater well-being.

Let's embark on this enlightening adventure together!

Chapter 2

Anatomy and Functions of the Vagus Nerve

The vagus nerve, also known as the 10th cranial nerve, is a fascinating and crucial component of the human nervous system. Stretching from the brainstem to the abdomen, this nerve plays a vital role in regulating numerous bodily functions, from heart rate and digestion to speech and breathing.

Let's delve into the intricate anatomy of the vagus nerve to better understand its structure and functions.

Starting at the brainstem, the vagus nerve emerges from the medulla oblongata and travels down towards the neck, serving as the longest and most complex of the cranial nerves. It is a mixed nerve, meaning it contains both sensory and motor fibers that transmit signals in two directions. The vagus nerve branches out extensively, forming connections with various organs and tissues throughout the body, making it a key player in the parasympathetic nervous system.

As the vagus nerve descends into the neck, it gives off several branches that innervate structures such as the larynx and pharynx, playing a crucial role in speech, swallowing, and vocalization. These branches also provide sensory feedback, allowing us to perceive sensations such as taste and touch in the throat and oral cavity.

Moving further down into the chest cavity, the vagus nerve continues its journey, branching out to innervate the heart and lungs. Through its connections with the cardiac plexus, the vagus nerve helps regulate heart rate and cardiac function, playing a vital role in maintaining cardiovascular homeostasis. Additionally, the nerve fibers that extend to the lungs contribute to the control of respiration, ensuring proper oxygen exchange and carbon dioxide elimination.

Descending into the abdomen, the vagus nerve forms connections with various organs of the gastrointestinal tract, including the stomach, liver, pancreas, and intestines. These connections are crucial for the regulation of digestion and nutrient absorption. The vagus nerve stimulates the release of digestive enzymes and controls processes such as peristalsis, which aids in the movement of food through the gastrointestinal tract.

Within the abdomen, the vagus nerve also plays a role in the gut-brain axis, facilitating communication between the digestive system and the central nervous system. This bidirectional communication is essential for regulating appetite, food intake, and the gut microbiome. Dysfunction of the vagus nerve can lead to digestive disorders such as gastroparesis, a condition characterized by delayed stomach emptying.

The vagus nerve also interacts with the autonomic nervous system, helping to maintain overall physiological balance in the body. As a major component of the parasympathetic nervous system, the vagus nerve counteracts the "fight or flight" response of the sympathetic nervous system, promoting rest, relaxation, and digestion. This delicate balance between the two branches of the autonomic nervous system is crucial for overall health and wellbeing.

In addition to its role in regulating physiological functions, the vagus nerve also plays a role in modulating emotional responses and stress. Known as the "wandering nerve," the vagus nerve has connections to various brain regions involved in emotional regulation, such as the amygdala and prefrontal cortex. Stimulation of the vagus nerve, through practices like deep breathing or meditation, can help promote relaxation and reduce stress.

Overall, the vagus nerve is a remarkable structure that exemplifies the intricate interconnectedness of the human body. Its far-reaching connections and multifaceted functions highlight the importance of this nerve in maintaining homeostasis and overall well-being. Understanding the detailed anatomy of the vagus nerve can shed light on its essential role in regulating vital bodily functions and supporting holistic health.

Primary Functions in the Body

The vagus nerve plays a crucial role in the body by connecting the brain to various organs and systems, helping to regulate important functions that keep us alive and well. Let's dive into the fascinating world of the vagus nerve and explore its primary functions in detail.

One of the key functions of the vagus nerve is its role in the parasympathetic nervous system, which is responsible for the body's rest and digest response. When activated, the vagus nerve promotes relaxation, slows down the heart rate, and enhances digestion by stimulating the release of gastric juices and enzymes. This helps the body to conserve energy and focus on processes like digestion and healing.

Furthermore, the vagus nerve plays a vital role in regulating the cardiovascular system. By innervating the heart, the vagus nerve helps to control heart rate and blood pressure, maintaining optimal cardiovascular function. When you take a deep breath and feel your heart rate slow down, you can thank the vagus nerve for its calming influence on the heart.

The vagus nerve is also involved in the communication between the gut and the brain, known as the gut-brain axis. This bi-directional connection allows the brain to influence gut function and vice versa. The vagus nerve transmits signals related to appetite, satiety, and digestion, playing a crucial role in the regulation of food intake and metabolism. It also helps to modulate emotions and mood through its connection with the brain, highlighting the intricate link between gut and brain health.

Another important function of the vagus nerve is its role in inflammation regulation. Through its anti-inflammatory effects, the vagus nerve helps to dampen the body's inflammatory response, reducing the risk of chronic inflammation and associated health conditions. This neuroimmune communication highlights the vagus nerve's ability to modulate the immune system and maintain immune balance within the body.

Furthermore, the vagus nerve is involved in the regulation of respiratory function. By innervating the muscles involved in breathing, the vagus nerve helps to control the rate and depth of respiration, ensuring proper oxygen exchange in the body. This function is essential for maintaining respiratory efficiency and overall health.

In addition to its physiological functions, the vagus nerve also plays a role in social engagement and emotional regulation. Known as the "social nerve," the vagus nerve is involved in facial expressions, vocalization, and eye contact, all of which are essential for social interactions and communication. The vagus nerve also helps to regulate emotional responses by modulating the release of neurotransmitters involved in mood regulation, such as serotonin and dopamine.

Overall, the vagus nerve is a multifaceted and essential component of the nervous system, with diverse functions that impact nearly every aspect of our health and well-being. From regulating the cardiovascular system and digestion to modulating inflammation and emotional responses, the vagus nerve plays a pivotal role in maintaining balance and harmony within the body.

As we continue to uncover the intricate connections between the vagus nerve and various bodily functions, we gain a deeper appreciation for the complexity and sophistication of our internal systems. The more we understand and support the functions of the vagus nerve, the better equipped we are to optimize our health and vitality.

What is Vagal Tone?

Throughout this book, you'll hear us referring to something called 'vagal tone.' So, before we delve in, let's define what it is.

Vagal tone is like the body's very own built-in chill pill. It's all about that vagus nerve, the longest cranial nerve in the body, which plays a key role in helping us stay calm, cool, and collected. Think of it as the conductor of the relaxation orchestra within us.

When our vagal tone is high, it's like having a soothing symphony playing in the background, keeping stress at bay and promoting a sense of well-being. On the flip side, a low vagal tone can make us feel more frazzled and on edge. So, it's no wonder that nurturing and boosting our vagal tone is a hot topic in the world of wellness and self-care.

In a nutshell, vagal tone is all about keeping our mind and body in harmony, like a peaceful duet that helps us navigate the ups and downs of life with grace and composure.

The Benefits of Working With the Vagus Nerve

Engaging with the vagus nerve can have a variety of benefits for your physical and mental health. Here's a detailed look:

- **Heart Health:** Stimulation of the vagus nerve can help to reduce heart rate and blood pressure, making it beneficial for heart health.

- **Digestive Efficiency:** It also positively influences the digestive system by improving gastric motility, which helps the body process and absorb nutrients effectively and ease various digestive disorders.

- **Reduced Inflammation:** By activating the vagus nerve, it's possible to reduce the levels of cytokines, which are inflammatory molecules, leading to decreased inflammation in the body.

- **Immunity Boost:** Enhanced vagal tone can lead to a better-functioning immune system, allowing the body to more effectively fight off infections and heal after injury.

- **Stress Reduction:** Regular engagement of the vagus nerve helps in the reduction of stress by controlling the body's relaxation response.

- **Anxiety and Depression:** Techniques that stimulate the vagus nerve have been shown to decrease symptoms of anxiety and depression due to their role in releasing mood-regulating neurotransmitters.

- **Better Sleep:** As it helps manage the body's relaxation response, it can also contribute to better sleep patterns and quality.

- **Increased Resilience:** Improved vagal tone can increase overall psychological and emotional resilience, helping to better manage emotional challenges.

- **Mind-Body Connection:** Working with the vagus nerve enhances the mind-body connection, aiding in greater awareness and presence.
- **Longevity:** There is some evidence suggesting that improved vagal tone is associated with greater longevity due to its positive effect on various body organs and systems.

When the Vagus Nerve Isn't Functioning Well ...

While the vagus nerve significantly contributes to well-functioning bodily systems, its impairment can lead to a cascade of health issues. Dysfunction in the vagus nerve can be typically linked to what's termed 'vagal tone'. A high vagal tone implies that the body can relax faster after stress - the desirable state. On the flip side, a low vagal tone is often associated with chronic stress, inflammation, and mood imbalances, among other issues.

Digestive Dilemmas:

Poor vagus nerve function can wreak havoc on the gut. It often presents as sluggish digestion, constipation, or gastroparesis—a condition where the stomach cannot empty properly. On the opposite spectrum, erratic signals can lead to cramps and irritable bowel syndrome. Consequently, if the maestro isn't cueing the orchestra properly, the symphony of digestion plays out of tune.

Cardiovascular Concerns:

In the cardiovascular realm, if the vagus nerve is underperforming, its capacity to control the heart rate is compromised. This inefficiency can heighten the risk of irregular heart rhythms and potentially increase stress on the heart. Moreover, it may affect blood pressure regulation, complicating cardiovascular health further.

Emotional Turbulence:

Mental health might take a hit as well if the vagal tone is low. Individuals might have a harder time managing stress, experience mood swings, or struggle with anxiety and depression. The calming influence the vagus nerve typically exerts fades, often leaving feelings of high tension in its absence.

Boosting Vagus Nerve Function

Given its significant impact, nurturing the health of the vagus nerve should be a prime focus for those looking toward holistic wellness.

Some ways to engage and stimulate this nerve include deep and slow breathing exercises, which promote relaxation and help to enhance vagal tone. Regular physical activity, another stimulant, naturally boosts the nerve's function while improving mood and digestion. Additionally, adopting tactics such as yoga and meditation has shown promising results in stress management and maintaining a good vagal tone. These are all things we're going to talk about in much more detail as we move through this book.

Put simply, the vagus nerve's role in sustaining good health cannot be overstated. It intricately connects multiple organs and systems, ensuring the body works not just as separate units but as a coherent, integrated ensemble.

Like a conductor leading an orchestra without drawing attention to itself, the vagus nerve supports and regulates key body functions quietly yet powerfully. To maintain this silent conductor in prime condition, embracing practices that support nerve health and reduce stress can be profoundly beneficial. Ultimately, a well-tuned vagus nerve sets the stage for a healthy, harmonious life—across both the physical and emotional realms.

What is the State of Your Vagus Nerve?

To help you understand how well your vagus nerve is functioning, let's try a quiz.

How would you describe your stress levels on a daily basis?

a) Low, I rarely feel stressed.

b) Moderate, I have some stressful moments but can manage them.

c) High, I often feel overwhelmed and stressed.

Do you experience any digestive issues, such as bloating, constipation, or diarrhea?

a) Rarely or never

b) Occasionally

c) Frequently

How well do you handle changes in temperature, such as going from a warm room to a cold room?

a) I adapt well without any issues.

b) I notice the change, but it doesn't affect me significantly.

c) I struggle to adjust and feel uncomfortable.

What is your sleep quality like?

a) I typically sleep well and wake up feeling rested.

b) I have trouble falling asleep or staying asleep occasionally.

c) I frequently have difficulty sleeping and wake up feeling tired.

How often do you practice relaxation techniques such as deep breathing, meditation, or yoga?

a) Daily

b) Occasionally

c) Rarely or never

Scoring:

- For every (a) answer, give yourself 1 point.
- For every (b) answer, give yourself 2 points.
- For every (c) answer, give yourself 3 points.

Interpretation:

- **5-8 points:** Your vagus nerve appears to be functioning well; keep up the good work maintaining your overall well-being!
- **9-12 points:** Your vagus nerve may be experiencing some challenges; consider incorporating more relaxation techniques and stress management strategies into your daily routine.
- **13-15 points:** Your vagus nerve could benefit from some extra care and attention. It's important to prioritize relaxation, stress reduction, and digestive health to support its function.

Remember, this quiz is just a fun way to gauge potential areas for improvement in your overall health and well-being. For any concerns about your vagus nerve or overall health, it's always best to consult with a healthcare professional.

Chapter 3

The Vagus Nerve and the Autonomic Nervous System

Because the nervous system is a complicated deal, let's dig even deeper than before. To truly understand the vagus nerve, we need to know about the autonomic nervous system in particular.

The autonomic nervous system is like the behind-the-scenes crew of your body, constantly working to keep things running smoothly without you even having to think about it. It's responsible for regulating all the automatic processes in your body, such as heart rate, digestion, breathing, and even bladder control.

Now, the autonomic nervous system has two main branches: the sympathetic nervous system and the parasympathetic nervous system. Think of them as the yin and yang of your body's internal control center.

The sympathetic nervous system is like your body's gas pedal. It kicks into gear in times of stress or danger, preparing you for fight or flight by increasing your heart rate, dilating your pupils, and releasing adrenaline to give you that extra boost of energy. It's like your body's own superhero, ready to jump into action when needed.

On the other hand, the parasympathetic nervous system is like your body's brake pedal. It helps you relax and rest after a stressful situation, slowing down your heart rate, constricting your pupils, and promoting digestion. It's like the calming voice in your head, telling you everything is going to be okay.

These two branches work together in a delicate balance, constantly adjusting and adapting to keep your body functioning properly. It's like a perfectly choreographed dance, with each branch taking the lead when needed and stepping back when not.

Now, here's where things get really interesting. Sometimes, the autonomic nervous system can get out of whack, causing problems like anxiety, high blood pressure, or digestive issues. This is where techniques like deep breathing, meditation, and exercise can help bring the system back into balance.

So, the next time you feel your heart racing or your stomach churning, remember that it's all thanks to your amazing autonomic nervous system working hard behind the scenes to keep you healthy and thriving.

In conclusion, the autonomic nervous system is like the unsung hero of your body, silently working to maintain harmony and balance in all your automatic bodily functions. It's a truly remarkable system that deserves recognition for all the hard work it does to keep you alive and well.

The Role of the Vagus Nerve in the Parasympathetic System

We know that the vagus nerve is the longest cranial nerve in the human body, extending from the brainstem all the way down to the abdomen, and it carries a plethora of essential information between the brain and various organs.

One of the most remarkable aspects of the vagus nerve is its bidirectional communication system. It not only transmits signals from the brain to the organs, but it also receives feedback from these organs, providing a continuous loop of information that helps maintain homeostasis within the body. This two-way communication allows the vagus nerve to finely tune the parasympathetic response as needed, adjusting heart rate, digestion, and other autonomic functions in response to different internal and external stimuli.

The vagus nerve is aptly named after the Latin word "vagus," meaning wandering, reflecting its extensive reach and ability to influence a wide array of bodily functions. It interacts with various organs, including the heart, lungs, liver, and intestines, exerting its influence through both the motor and sensory fibers it contains. By releasing acetylcholine, a neurotransmitter that promotes relaxation and restorative processes, the vagus nerve helps to counterbalance the sympathetic nervous system's fight-or-flight response, promoting a state of rest and digest.

One of the vagus nerve's primary functions is to lower heart rate and blood pressure during times of relaxation. This helps conserve energy and promote efficient digestion by diverting blood flow to the digestive organs. Additionally, the vagus nerve stimulates the release of digestive enzymes and promotes the peristaltic movement of the intestines, aiding in the absorption of nutrients and the elimination of waste.

But the role of the vagus nerve doesn't stop at digestion and heart rate regulation. It also plays a crucial role in modulating inflammation and immune responses. Through its anti-inflammatory effects, the vagus nerve helps regulate the body's response to stress and injury, promoting healing and reducing the risk of chronic inflammatory conditions. This neuro-immune communication highlights the intricate link between the nervous and immune systems, with the vagus nerve serving as a key mediator of this cross-talk.

Furthermore, the vagus nerve is closely involved in regulating mood and emotional responses. Its connections to various brain regions, including the amygdala and prefrontal cortex, enable it to influence emotional processing and stress responses. By dampening the body's stress response and promoting feelings of calm and relaxation, the vagus nerve contributes to emotional well-being and resilience in the face of life's challenges.

In addition to its role in physiological functions, the vagus nerve has been a subject of interest in the field of bioelectronic medicine. Researchers have explored the potential of vagus nerve stimulation as a therapeutic intervention for a variety of conditions, including epilepsy, depression, and inflammatory disorders. By modulating the activity of the vagus nerve through electrical stimulation, clinicians aim to restore balance to the autonomic nervous system and alleviate symptoms associated with these conditions.

Achieving Balance Between the Sympathetic and Parasympathetic Systems

Achieving the balance between the sympathetic and parasympathetic nervous systems is crucial for maintaining overall well-being and optimal functioning.

These two systems work together to regulate our body's responses to stress and relaxation, with the sympathetic system responsible for the "fight or flight" response and the parasympathetic system for the "rest and digest" response. Finding harmony between these two systems is key to living a healthy and balanced life.

Let's start by diving into the sympathetic nervous system, often referred to as our body's "gas pedal." When we perceive a threat or are faced with a stressful situation, the sympathetic system kicks into gear, releasing adrenaline and triggering a cascade of physiological responses designed to help us either fight the threat or run away from it. Our heart rate increases, our breathing becomes faster and shallower, and our muscles tense up in preparation for action.

While the sympathetic system is essential for our survival, chronic activation can lead to negative health consequences, including increased risk of heart disease, anxiety, and weakened immune function. This is where the parasympathetic nervous system, our body's "brake pedal," comes into play. This system helps counterbalance the effects of stress by promoting relaxation, aiding digestion, and restoring our body to a state of calm.

Achieving balance between these two systems requires a multi-faceted approach that addresses both physical and mental aspects of well-being. Here are some strategies to help you find harmony between your sympathetic and parasympathetic systems:

- **Mindfulness practices:** Mindfulness techniques, such as meditation, deep breathing, and body scans, can help activate the parasympathetic system and promote feelings of relaxation and calm. Taking a few minutes each day to engage in mindfulness practices can help reduce stress levels and improve overall well-being.
- **Physical activity:** Regular exercise is a powerful tool for achieving balance between the sympathetic and parasympathetic systems. Exercise helps to release pent-up energy and tension while also promoting relaxation and reducing cortisol levels. Find a physical activity that you enjoy, whether it's yoga, jogging, or dancing, and make it a regular part of your routine.
- **Healthy eating habits:** Eating a balanced diet rich in whole foods, fruits, vegetables, and lean proteins can support the functioning of both the sympathetic and parasympathetic systems. Avoiding excessive caffeine and sugar can help prevent spikes in cortisol levels and promote a more stable mood and energy throughout the day.
- **Quality sleep:** Getting enough restful sleep is essential for maintaining a healthy balance between the sympathetic and parasympathetic systems. Aim for 7-9 hours of sleep each night and establish a bedtime routine that promotes relaxation, such as

reading a book, taking a warm bath, or practicing gentle yoga poses.

- **Stress management techniques**: Finding healthy ways to cope with stress can help prevent chronic activation of the sympathetic nervous system. Try incorporating stress-reducing activities into your daily routine, such as spending time in nature, journaling, or connecting with loved ones.

- **Self-care practices:** Taking time for yourself and engaging in activities that bring you joy and relaxation can help nurture your parasympathetic system. Whether it's enjoying a bubble bath, practicing a hobby, or going for a leisurely walk, prioritize self-care to support your overall well-being.

By implementing these strategies and prioritizing balance between the sympathetic and parasympathetic systems, you can cultivate a sense of harmony in your mind and body. Remember that achieving balance is an ongoing process that requires self-awareness, patience, and dedication. By taking small steps each day towards promoting relaxation and reducing stress, you can create a life that is healthy, vibrant, and grounded in tranquility.

From this point on, let's start looking at how the vagus nerve can help with various issues and what you can do to help the process along. Let's start with improving mental health.

Chapter 4

The Vagus Nerve and Mental Health

In this chapter, we will delve into the intricate web of connections between the vagus nerve and mental health, unraveling the mysteries behind its profound influence on our well-being.

Through its bidirectional communication with the brain, the vagus nerve acts as a conduit for signals that impact our mood, cognition, and behavior. From calming our fight-or-flight response to fostering feelings of connection and empathy, this enigmatic nerve holds the key to understanding the mind-body connection like never before.

Influence on Mood and Emotional Regulation

As the 10th cranial nerve, the vagus nerve is a key player in our body's ability to regulate emotions and mood. It plays a significant role in the communication between the brain and the body, promoting a sense of well-being and emotional stability.

One of the vagus nerve's primary roles is in regulating the parasympathetic nervous system, which is responsible for the body's rest-and-digest response. When activated, the vagus nerve helps to calm the body by slowing down heart rate, relaxing muscles, and stimulating the release of feel-good hormones like oxytocin and dopamine. This activation is crucial for reducing stress and promoting relaxation, which is essential for maintaining a healthy emotional balance.

Research has shown that individuals with a strong vagal tone, meaning their vagus nerve is functioning optimally, tend to have better emotional regulation and resilience to stress. A higher vagal tone is associated with improved mood, greater emotional stability, and increased overall well-being. On the other hand, low vagal tone has been linked to conditions such as depression, anxiety, and mood disorders.

One of the ways the vagus nerve influences mood and emotional regulation is through its connection to the brain's limbic system, which is responsible for processing emotions. The vagus nerve sends signals to the amygdala, the brain's fear center, to help regulate the intensity of emotional responses. By modulating the activity of the amygdala, the vagus nerve helps us navigate through challenging situations without becoming overwhelmed by fear or anxiety.

Moreover, the vagus nerve plays a crucial role in the body's stress response system. When we encounter stressful situations, the vagus nerve helps to regulate the release of cortisol, the stress hormone. By promoting relaxation and calming the body's stress response, the vagus nerve helps to prevent the negative effects of chronic stress on mood and emotional well-being.

Furthermore, the vagus nerve influences the production of neurotransmitters such as serotonin and GABA, which are essential for regulating mood and emotions. Serotonin, often referred to as the "happiness hormone," is involved in mood regulation, while GABA is a calming neurotransmitter that helps to reduce anxiety and promote relaxation. The vagus nerve plays a role in the synthesis and release of these neurotransmitters, contributing to emotional balance and mental well-being.

In addition to its direct influence on emotional regulation, the vagus nerve also plays a role in social bonding and connection. Oxytocin, often referred to as the "love hormone," is released in response to positive social interactions such as hugging or connecting with loved ones. The vagus nerve helps to stimulate the release of oxytocin, promoting feelings of trust, bonding, and emotional connection.

Practices that stimulate and strengthen the vagus nerve can be beneficial for enhancing mood and emotional regulation. Mindfulness meditation, deep breathing exercises, yoga, and acupuncture are all techniques that have been shown to activate the vagus nerve and improve vagal tone. These practices help to promote relaxation, reduce stress, and enhance emotional well-being by supporting the optimal functioning of the vagus nerve.

Moreover, physical activity has been found to be beneficial for vagal tone and emotional regulation. Regular exercise helps to stimulate the vagus nerve, promoting relaxation and reducing stress levels. Activities such as walking, running, and swimming can all help to enhance vagal tone and improve mood by supporting the body's natural stress response system.

The diet also plays a role in supporting the vagus nerve and emotional well-being. Consuming a diet rich in omega-3 fatty acids, antioxidants, and fiber can help to reduce inflammation in the body, which can impact vagal tone. Foods such as fatty fish, nuts, seeds, fruits, and vegetables can all support the health of the vagus nerve and contribute to better mood and emotional regulation.

Connection to Anxiety, Depression, and Stress

First off, picture the vagus nerve as a major highway that runs from the brainstem down to the abdomen, touching various major organs along the way. It plays a key role in the parasympathetic nervous system, which is responsible for the body's rest and digest responses. When stimulated, the vagus nerve acts like a calming agent, helping to regulate heart rate, digestion, and even mood.

Anxiety, that feeling of unease or worry, can be linked to an overactive vagus nerve. When the vagus nerve is in hyperdrive, it can lead to an imbalance in the body's stress response system. This can result in heightened feelings of anxiety as the body struggles to modulate its stress levels. People experiencing chronic anxiety may have an overly sensitive vagus nerve, which can exacerbate their symptoms.

On the flip side, depression, a mood disorder characterized by persistent feelings of sadness and hopelessness, can also be influenced by the vagus nerve. Studies have shown that individuals with depression often have reduced vagal tone, meaning their vagus nerve isn't functioning as effectively in regulating mood and emotions. This can contribute to a sense of emotional dysregulation and make it harder for individuals to bounce back from negative experiences.

Now, let's talk about stress, that all-too-familiar feeling of being overwhelmed by life's demands. The vagus nerve serves as a key player in the body's stress response system, helping to signal when it's time to relax and unwind. However, chronic stress can lead to vagal tone imbalance, affecting the nerve's ability to properly regulate stress levels. This can create a vicious cycle where heightened stress levels further impact the vagus nerve, perpetuating feelings of anxiety and depression.

Overall, the vagus nerve plays a crucial role in our emotional well-being, with strong connections to anxiety, depression, and stress. By understanding how this nerve operates and incorporating practices that support its function, you can take proactive steps towards promoting a healthier mind and body. Remember, your vagus nerve is a powerful ally in the battle against negative emotions; treat it well, and it will reward you with a greater sense of calm and resilience.

How to Use the Vagus Nerve to Improve Mental Health

In recent years, researchers and healthcare professionals have been exploring how stimulating and nurturing the vagus nerve can have a positive impact on mental health. By understanding how the vagus nerve works and incorporating specific techniques into your daily routine, you can potentially improve your overall mental well-being.

One of the key ways to work with the vagus nerve to enhance mental health is through techniques that focus on stimulating the nerve's functioning. These techniques can range from simple breathing exercises to more advanced biofeedback methods.

Let's delve into some actionable strategies that you can incorporate into your daily routine to tap into the power of the vagus nerve for better mental health.

Deep Breathing Exercises:

One of the most effective ways to stimulate the vagus nerve is through deep breathing exercises. By taking slow, deep breaths, you can activate the parasympathetic nervous system, which is responsible for promoting relaxation and reducing stress.

Start by finding a quiet and comfortable place to sit or lie down. Inhale deeply through your nose for a count of four, hold your breath for a moment, and then exhale slowly through your mouth for a count of six. Repeat this process several times, focusing on the sensation of your breath entering and leaving your body. This simple yet powerful technique can help calm your mind and body, promoting a sense of inner peace and well-being.

Cold Exposure

Another effective way to stimulate the vagus nerve is through cold exposure. Cold showers or immersing yourself in cold water can activate the body's "fight or flight" response, triggering the vagus nerve to kick in and help regulate your autonomic nervous system. Start by gradually exposing yourself to cold temperatures, whether through cold showers, ice baths, or simply splashing cold water on your face.

The shock of cold can stimulate the vagus nerve and promote a sense of alertness and mental clarity. Over time, regular cold exposure can potentially improve your resilience to stress and enhance your mental health.

Yoga and Meditation

Practices like yoga and meditation have been shown to have a positive impact on mental health by calming the mind and body and promoting relaxation. Certain yoga poses and meditation techniques specifically target the vagus nerve, helping to regulate the heart rate and promote a sense of tranquility. Incorporate yoga poses like Fish Pose, Cobra Pose, and Lion's Breath into your practice to stimulate the vagus nerve and promote relaxation.

Fish Pose:

- Start by lying flat on your back on the yoga mat with your legs extended and your arms resting by your sides.
- Bring your hands palms down underneath your hips, with your elbows tucked in close to your body.

- Press your forearms and elbows into the mat as you inhale and gently arch your back, lifting your chest and upper body off the mat.
- Rest the top of your head lightly on the mat, allowing your neck to gently arch back.
- Keep your legs and feet active by pressing them into the mat.
- Hold the pose for 5–10 breaths, breathing deeply and focusing on opening the heart center.
- To come out of the pose, gently release the head back to the mat and lower your chest back down.
- Remove your hands from under your hips and rest in Corpse Pose (Savasana) for a few breaths to relax and integrate the pose.

Remember to listen to your body and only go as far into the pose as feels comfortable for you.

Cobra Pose:

- Start by lying flat on your stomach on your mat, with your legs straight and your feet hip-width apart. Place your palms on the mat under your shoulders, with your elbows close to your torso.
- Inhale deeply and press the tops of your feet, thighs, and pelvis into the mat while keeping your pubic bone grounded.

- On your next inhale, slowly begin to straighten your arms, lifting your chest off the mat. Keep your elbows slightly bent, and draw your shoulder blades together and down your back.
- Ensure that your gaze is forward, your neck is in line with your spine, and your chin is slightly tucked.
- Take deep breaths as you hold the pose, feeling a gentle stretch in your back and abdomen. Avoid putting too much pressure on your hands; use the strength of your back muscles to lift yourself.
- To come out of the pose, exhale slowly and lower your chest back down to the mat, releasing any tension in your body.
- Repeat the Cobra Pose a few times, focusing on your breath and maintaining proper alignment. Listen to your body and adjust the pose as needed to suit your comfort level.

Remember to warm up your body before attempting any yoga poses, and always listen to your body to prevent injury.

Lion's Breath:

- Find a comfortable seated position on your mat. You can sit cross-legged or on your knees, whichever is more comfortable for you.

- Place your hands on your knees or thighs, palms facing down.
- Take a deep inhale through your nose, filling your lungs with air. Feel your belly rise as you breathe in.
- As you exhale, open your mouth wide, stick out your tongue, and exhale forcefully, making a "ha" sound. Imagine you are trying to fog up a mirror with your breath.
- While exhaling, also gaze towards the space between your eyebrows (your third eye) or up towards the ceiling, if that feels comfortable for you.
- As you exhale, try to release any tension in your face, jaw, shoulders, and throat. Let go of any stress or negative energy with each Lion's Breath.
- Repeat this breathing exercise 3-5 times, or as many times as you feel comfortable.
- After completing the Lion's Breath, take a moment to notice how you feel. You may feel more relaxed, energized, or centered.

Remember to listen to your body and only practice Lion's Breath as much as feels comfortable for you.

Additionally, mindfulness meditation, focusing on the present moment, and observing your thoughts without judgment can help activate the vagus nerve and reduce symptoms of anxiety and depression.

Social Connections

The vagus nerve is also closely linked to social connections and human bonding. Engaging in meaningful and positive social interactions can help stimulate the vagus nerve and promote emotional well-being. Make an effort to nurture your relationships with friends, family, and loved ones, whether through face-to-face conversations, phone calls, or virtual meet-ups.

Connecting with others can help increase feelings of safety and trust, activating the vagus nerve's "rest and digest" response and promoting a sense of calm and contentment.

Laughter and Play

Laughter has been shown to have a profound impact on mental health, releasing endorphins and reducing stress levels. Engaging in activities that bring joy and laughter, such as watching a funny movie, playing with pets, or engaging in playful interactions, can help stimulate the vagus nerve and enhance your mood.

Try incorporating more moments of laughter and playfulness into your daily routine to boost your mental well-being and activate the vagus nerve's relaxation response.

Chapter 5

The Vagus Nerve and Physical Health

We know that the vagus nerve, a crucial part of the parasympathetic nervous system, plays a significant role in regulating various bodily functions such as heart rate, digestion, and inflammation. In recent years, researchers have uncovered the profound impact that stimulating the vagus nerve can have on improving overall health.

Whether you are seeking relief from chronic pain, looking to boost your immune system, or simply hoping to enhance your overall well-being, harnessing the power of the vagus nerve can offer a wealth of benefits.

Impact on Cardiovascular Health

The vagus nerve has two main branches, the left vagus nerve and the right vagus nerve, which innervate different regions of the body. The right vagus nerve primarily influences the sinoatrial (SA) node, while the left vagus nerve predominantly affects the atrioventricular (AV) node. These two branches work together to regulate heart rate, blood pressure, and heart rhythm, among other cardiovascular functions.

One of the key ways in which the vagus nerve can help improve cardiovascular health is through its role in regulating heart rate. The vagus nerve acts as a brake on the heart, slowing down the heart rate when the body is at rest or under low stress. This parasympathetic activity helps maintain healthy heart rate variability, which is a strong indicator of cardiovascular health. Individuals with higher heart rate variability are often more resilient to stress and have a lower risk of developing cardiovascular disease.

In addition to regulating heart rate, the vagus nerve also plays a crucial role in controlling blood pressure. When the body is under stress or in a fight-or-flight response, the sympathetic nervous system is activated, causing an increase in heart rate and blood pressure. The vagus nerve, through its parasympathetic activity, helps counteract this response by promoting relaxation and lowering blood pressure. By activating the vagus nerve through various techniques, such as deep breathing exercises or biofeedback, individuals can help maintain healthy blood pressure levels and reduce the risk of hypertension.

Moreover, the vagus nerve is involved in the regulation of heart rhythm, particularly through its modulation of the SA and AV nodes. By influencing the electrical signals that control the heart's contractions, the vagus nerve helps maintain a regular and coordinated heart rhythm. When the vagus nerve is functioning optimally, the risk of arrhythmias, such as atrial fibrillation, is reduced. Studies have shown that enhancing vagal tone, or the strength of vagus nerve activity, can help prevent the occurrence of various heart rhythm disorders.

Another fascinating aspect of the vagus nerve is its role in reducing inflammation throughout the body. Chronic inflammation is a known risk factor for cardiovascular disease, as it can damage blood vessels and promote the development of atherosclerosis. The vagus nerve exerts anti-inflammatory effects through its release of neurotransmitters, such as acetylcholine, which inhibits the production of pro-inflammatory cytokines. By activating the vagus nerve, either through methods like meditation or vagus nerve stimulation, individuals can help mitigate inflammation and protect their cardiovascular health.

Furthermore, the vagus nerve is involved in the regulation of the gastrointestinal system, which has a direct impact on cardiovascular health. The gut-brain axis, a complex communication network between the brain and the digestive system, is partially mediated by the vagus nerve. A healthy gut microbiome, influenced by vagal activity, can produce beneficial metabolites that reduce cardiovascular risk factors, such as cholesterol levels and blood sugar regulation. By promoting gut health through diet and lifestyle choices that support vagal function, individuals can positively impact their cardiovascular health.

In recent years, research has highlighted the potential therapeutic applications of vagus nerve stimulation for improving cardiovascular health. Vagus nerve stimulation involves the targeted delivery of electrical impulses to the vagus nerve, which can modulate its activity and influence various physiological processes. Clinical studies have shown promising results in using vagus nerve stimulation to treat heart failure, hypertension, and other cardiovascular conditions, demonstrating the therapeutic potential of harnessing the power of this nerve.

Role in Digestion and Gut Health

The vagus nerve plays a crucial role in the digestive process by regulating key functions such as swallowing, digestion, and nutrient absorption. When we consume food, sensory information is relayed to the brain via the vagus nerve, which then signals the release of digestive enzymes and hormones to facilitate proper digestion.

One of the most significant ways in which the vagus nerve impacts digestive health is through its role in the "rest and digest" response of the parasympathetic nervous system. When the body is in a state of relaxation, the vagus nerve stimulates the release of digestive juices in the stomach, enhances intestinal motility, and promotes nutrient absorption. This ensures that our bodies can efficiently break down food and extract essential nutrients to support overall health.

Furthermore, the vagus nerve communicates with the enteric nervous system, sometimes referred to as the "second brain," which is a complex network of neurons found in the gastrointestinal tract. This intricate communication network helps regulate gut motility, the secretion of digestive enzymes, and the maintenance of a healthy gut microbiome.

Gut-Brain Axis and the Vagus Nerve

The connection between the gut and the brain, often referred to as the gut-brain axis, is a bidirectional communication network that involves the vagus nerve as a central player. Research has shown that the vagus nerve plays a crucial role in transmitting signals between the gut and the brain, influencing various aspects of health, including mood, cognition, and immune function.

In recent years, there has been growing interest in the impact of the gut-brain axis on overall well-being, with studies highlighting the role of the vagus nerve in regulating gut health and influencing mental health conditions such as anxiety and depression. By maintaining a healthy gut environment through proper digestion and nutrient absorption, the vagus nerve can help support optimal brain function and emotional well-being.

Vagus Nerve Stimulation and Gut Health

In addition to its natural functions, the vagus nerve can also be stimulated artificially through techniques such as vagus nerve stimulation (VNS). VNS is a therapeutic approach that involves sending electrical impulses to the vagus nerve to treat various conditions, including epilepsy, depression, and inflammatory disorders.

Recent research has also explored the potential benefits of vagus nerve stimulation for promoting gut health and alleviating digestive disorders such as irritable bowel syndrome (IBS) and inflammatory bowel disease (IBD). By modulating the activity of the vagus nerve, researchers believe that VNS may help regulate gut inflammation, restore gut motility, and rebalance the gut microbiome, thereby improving overall digestive health.

Lifestyle Factors and Vagus Nerve Function

While the vagus nerve plays a significant role in digestive health, its function can be influenced by various lifestyle factors. Practices such as deep breathing, meditation, and yoga have been shown to stimulate the vagus nerve and promote relaxation, which can in turn enhance digestion and gut function.

Furthermore, maintaining a healthy diet rich in fiber, probiotics, and prebiotics can support a thriving gut microbiome and optimize vagus nerve function. By nourishing the gut with a diverse array of nutrients, you can help ensure that the vagus nerve and the enteric nervous system work synergistically to support optimal digestive health.

Effects on Immune Response and Inflammation

The vagus nerve plays a significant role in regulating various bodily functions, including digestion, heart rate, and even our immune response.

One of the key ways in which the vagus nerve influences the immune response is through a process known as the "cholinergic anti-inflammatory pathway." When the body encounters a threat, such as an infection or injury, immune cells release pro-inflammatory molecules to help combat the invader. However, excessive inflammation can lead to tissue damage and contribute to the development of chronic conditions like autoimmune diseases.

Here's where the vagus nerve steps in as a powerful mediator of inflammation. By releasing acetylcholine, a neurotransmitter that activates the cholinergic anti-inflammatory pathway, the vagus nerve can dampen the immune response and help maintain balance in the inflammatory process. This mechanism acts as a feedback loop, preventing excessive inflammation and promoting tissue repair once the threat has been neutralized.

Research has shown that stimulating the vagus nerve, either through techniques like deep breathing, meditation, or devices such as vagus nerve stimulators, can have profound effects on the immune response. By activating the cholinergic anti-inflammatory pathway, these interventions can help reduce inflammation, improve immune function, and support overall well-being.

Furthermore, the vagus nerve's influence on inflammation goes beyond just the immune system. It also plays a role in regulating the gut-brain axis – the bidirectional communication between the gut and the brain. This communication pathway is essential for maintaining gut health and influencing mood, cognition, and even immune function.

In addition to its anti-inflammatory effects, the vagus nerve can modulate the release of stress hormones like cortisol, which can impact immune function. Chronic stress can dysregulate the immune response, leading to increased inflammation and vulnerability to infections. By activating the vagus nerve through relaxation techniques or other interventions, we can help mitigate the detrimental effects of stress on the immune system.

It's important to note that individual differences in vagal tone—the strength of the vagus nerve's influence on bodily functions – can impact how effectively the immune response is regulated. Factors like genetics, lifestyle, and environmental influences can all play a role in determining vagal tone and, consequently, immune function.

Overall, the vagus nerve's effects on immune response and inflammation highlight the intricate interplay between the nervous system, the immune system, and overall health. By understanding and leveraging the power of the vagus nerve, we can support our immune system, reduce inflammation, and promote greater well-being.

On the other hand, if this important nerve isn't functioning well, it can have a significant impact on inflammation and the immune system.

When the vagus nerve isn't working properly, this regulation can be disrupted, leading to an overactive inflammatory response. This can contribute to various health issues, such as chronic inflammation, which in turn can weaken the immune system's ability to fight off infections and diseases.

So, it's safe to say that keeping our vagus nerve in tip-top shape is key to maintaining a well-balanced immune system and preventing inflammation from going haywire.

Vagus Nerve Strategies to Improve Physical Health

When it comes to optimizing physical health, tapping into the power of the vagus nerve can be a game-changer. By incorporating specific practices and lifestyle habits that activate the vagus nerve, you can significantly boost your physical health.

In our last section, we talked about yoga, deep breathing, and cold exposure, and these are things that can help with physical health too. However, there are a few extra strategies to add to your list.

So, here are actionable strategies to harness the potential of the vagus nerve for better overall well-being:

Regular Exercise

Engage in regular physical activity to support optimal vagal tone and overall physical health. Aim for a combination of cardiovascular exercise, strength training, and flexibility exercises to keep your body strong and resilient. Exercise has been shown to increase heart rate variability, an indicator of vagal tone.

Consider incorporating activities like yoga, Pilates, or tai chi into your workout routine. These mind-body practices are not only great for physical fitness but also help promote relaxation and activate the vagus nerve. Find a form of exercise that you enjoy and make it a regular part of your routine.

Proper Nutrition

Fuel your body with a balanced diet rich in nutrients that support vagal function and overall physical health. Include foods high in omega-3 fatty acids, such as fatty fish, flaxseeds, and walnuts, which can help reduce inflammation and support brain health, including vagal tone.

Make sure to stay hydrated throughout the day by drinking an adequate amount of water. Dehydration can negatively impact vagal function and overall energy levels. Aim to drink at least 8–10 glasses of water daily to keep your body hydrated and functioning optimally.

Mindful Eating

Practice mindful eating to support digestion and activate the vagus nerve's role in the gut-brain connection. Take the time to savor each bite, chew your food slowly, and pay attention to your body's hunger and fullness cues. Mindful eating can help reduce stress and promote optimal digestion.

Consider incorporating foods that are known to support gut health, such as fermented foods like yogurt, kefir, and kimchi. These foods contain probiotics that can help maintain a healthy balance of gut bacteria, which is essential for vagal function and overall digestive health.

Quality Sleep

Prioritize getting an adequate amount of quality sleep each night to support vagal tone and overall physical recovery. Create a bedtime routine that helps signal to your body that it's time to wind down, such as dimming the lights, disconnecting from screens, and practicing relaxation techniques like deep breathing or gentle stretching.

Aim for 7-9 hours of quality sleep per night to allow your body to repair and rejuvenate. Poor sleep can negatively impact vagal function and contribute to various health issues, so make sleep a priority for optimal physical health.

By implementing these actionable strategies and incorporating vagus nerve-stimulating practices into your daily routine, you can harness the power of this vital nerve to enhance your physical health and overall well-being.

Remember that consistency is key, so start small and gradually incorporate these habits into your lifestyle to reap the full benefits. Prioritize self-care, listen to your body, and enjoy the journey to improved physical health through the activation of the vagus nerve.

Chapter 6

The Vagus Nerve and Chronic Illness

What's next? Well, in this chapter, we will delve into the intricate web of connections between the vagus nerve and chronic illnesses.

Recent research has shed light on the link between the vagus nerve and chronic illnesses such as autoimmune disorders, depression, and even gastrointestinal issues. By understanding the mechanisms through which the vagus nerve impacts these conditions, we gain valuable insight into potential therapeutic interventions and lifestyle changes that can make a tangible difference in our health outcomes.

By understanding all of this, you can start to make changes that may bring you relief from troublesome symptoms.

Connection to Chronic Pain and Fibromyalgia

Did you know that the vagus nerve also has a significant impact on chronic pain conditions like fibromyalgia?

Chronic pain is a complex and debilitating condition that affects millions of people worldwide. Fibromyalgia, in particular, is a chronic pain disorder characterized by widespread musculoskeletal pain, fatigue, and tenderness in specific areas of the body. While the exact cause of fibromyalgia is still unknown, researchers have identified a strong link between the vagus nerve and the development of chronic pain conditions.

One of the key ways in which the vagus nerve influences chronic pain is through its role in regulating inflammation. We know that inflammation is the body's natural response to injury or illness, but when it becomes chronic, it can contribute to the development of pain and other symptoms associated with conditions like fibromyalgia. The vagus nerve helps to modulate inflammation by releasing neurotransmitters like acetylcholine, which have anti-inflammatory effects.

Additionally, the vagus nerve is involved in the body's stress response system, known as the HPA axis. Chronic stress can trigger inflammation and exacerbate pain symptoms in conditions like fibromyalgia. The vagus nerve plays a crucial role in regulating the body's stress response by influencing the release of cortisol, a hormone involved in the body's response to stress. When the vagus nerve is not functioning properly, it can lead to dysregulation of the HPA axis, contributing to the development of chronic pain conditions.

Furthermore, the vagus nerve is also connected to the brain's limbic system, which is responsible for processing emotions and sensations. Dysfunction in the vagus nerve can disrupt the communication between the brain and the body, leading to alterations in pain perception and sensory processing. This can contribute to the development of hypersensitivity to pain in conditions like fibromyalgia.

Research has shown that individuals with fibromyalgia often have decreased vagal tone, which refers to the strength and efficiency of the signals sent by the vagus nerve. Low vagal tone has been associated with increased inflammation, heightened stress responses, and alterations in pain processing, all of which can contribute to the development and maintenance of chronic pain conditions.

By understanding the connection between the vagus nerve and chronic pain, we can explore new avenues for managing and treating these complex conditions. Through lifestyle modifications, mind-body practices, and targeted interventions, we can improve vagal tone, reduce inflammation, and alleviate pain symptoms, leading to a better quality of life.

The Vagus Nerve's Role in Autoimmune Diseases

The vagus nerve plays a fascinating and increasingly appreciated role in autoimmune diseases. We know that one of its key functions is to regulate the body's inflammatory response, which is crucial to maintaining immune balance. In recent years, researchers have discovered that the vagus nerve can act as a powerful modulator of the immune system, impacting the development and progression of autoimmune diseases.

Autoimmune diseases occur when the body's immune system mistakenly attacks its own tissues and organs, leading to chronic inflammation and tissue damage. Conditions such as rheumatoid arthritis, lupus, Crohn's disease, and multiple sclerosis are just a few examples of autoimmune diseases that can have debilitating effects on individuals. The intricate interplay between the immune system and the vagus nerve has provided new insights into the mechanisms underlying these conditions.

The vagus nerve exerts its influence on the immune system through a process known as the cholinergic anti-inflammatory pathway. This pathway involves the release of acetylcholine, a neurotransmitter that activates receptors on immune cells, leading to the suppression of pro-inflammatory cytokines and the promotion of anti-inflammatory responses. By dampening the immune response in this manner, the vagus nerve helps to prevent excessive inflammation and tissue damage. However, in the context of autoimmune diseases, dysregulation of this pathway can result in unchecked inflammation and immune dysregulation.

Research has shown that dysfunction of the vagus nerve and the cholinergic anti-inflammatory pathway can contribute to the development and progression of autoimmune diseases. For example, in rheumatoid arthritis, a chronic inflammatory condition affecting the joints, impaired vagus nerve function has been implicated in promoting joint inflammation and tissue destruction. Studies have demonstrated that stimulating the vagus nerve through techniques such as vagus nerve stimulation (VNS) or bioelectronic devices can potentially reduce inflammation and alleviate symptoms in rheumatoid arthritis patients.

Similarly, in systemic lupus erythematosus (SLE), an autoimmune disease characterized by widespread inflammation and organ damage, abnormalities in vagus nerve signaling have been observed. Dysfunctional vagus nerve activity may exacerbate the inflammatory response in SLE, contributing to disease flares and tissue damage. By targeting the vagus nerve with therapeutic interventions, such as VNS or pharmacological agents that enhance vagal tone, researchers aim to modulate the immune response and improve outcomes for individuals with SLE.

Crohn's disease, a chronic inflammatory bowel disorder, also showcases the intricate relationship between the vagus nerve and autoimmune diseases. Dysfunction of the vagus nerve can disrupt the balance between pro-inflammatory and anti-inflammatory signaling in the gut, leading to intestinal inflammation and symptoms characteristic of Crohn's disease. Therapeutic strategies aimed at restoring vagus nerve function in Crohn's disease patients may hold promise for attenuating inflammation and improving gastrointestinal health.

Multiple sclerosis (MS), a progressive autoimmune disorder affecting the central nervous system, highlights the role of the vagus nerve in modulating neuroinflammation. Studies have revealed that vagus nerve stimulation can reduce inflammatory responses in the brain and spinal cord in animal models of MS, suggesting a potential therapeutic approach for managing disease progression in MS patients. By harnessing the anti-inflammatory properties of the vagus nerve, researchers are exploring novel treatment strategies for autoimmune conditions that impact the nervous system.

In addition to its direct effects on immune function, the vagus nerve is also implicated in the regulation of the gut-brain axis, a bidirectional communication system between the gastrointestinal tract and the brain. The gut microbiota, which plays a crucial role in immune regulation and inflammation, can influence vagal signaling and immune responses. Dysbiosis, or an imbalance in the gut microbiota, has been associated with autoimmune diseases and may impact vagus nerve function. Strategies to modulate the gut microbiota, such as probiotics and dietary interventions, could potentially enhance vagal tone and mitigate inflammation in autoimmune conditions.

By understanding and harnessing the mechanisms by which the vagus nerve regulates immune responses, researchers are paving the way for innovative therapeutic approaches to manage autoimmune diseases. From rheumatoid arthritis to lupus, Crohn's disease to multiple sclerosis, the vagus nerve's role in autoimmune diseases offers new avenues for intervention and hope for individuals living with these challenging conditions.

As research continues to unravel the complexities of this dynamic interplay, the potential for targeted therapies that harness the power of the vagus nerve to modulate immune responses and mitigate inflammation is increasingly promising.

Vagal Nerve Stimulation as a Treatment Option

Vagus nerve stimulation (VNS) has garnered increasing interest in the medical field for its potential therapeutic benefits in treating various conditions such as fibromyalgia, chronic pain, and autoimmune diseases. By modulating the activity of the vagus nerve through stimulation, it is believed that people suffering from these conditions may experience relief and improvement in their symptoms.

However, it's important to remember that you shouldn't make any changes to your lifestyle or medication routine without speaking to your doctor first. Always check in with your medical team to ensure that you're getting the very best treatment for your condition. Everyone is different, and there is no one-size-fits-all approach here.

Understanding Vagus Nerve Stimulation (VNS)

Before delving into the specific benefits of VNS for fibromyalgia, chronic pain, and autoimmune diseases, it's important to understand how this therapy works.

Vagus nerve stimulation involves sending electrical impulses to the vagus nerve, which then communicates with the brain and various organs to regulate functions such as heart rate, digestion, inflammation, and pain perception. By modulating the activity of the vagus nerve, VNS can influence the body's response to stress, inflammation, and pain.

VNS for Fibromyalgia

Fibromyalgia is a chronic condition characterized by widespread musculoskeletal pain, fatigue, and heightened sensitivity to pain. Research suggests that VNS may be beneficial for individuals with fibromyalgia by modulating pain signals and reducing inflammation. By stimulating the vagus nerve, VNS can help regulate the body's pain response and potentially alleviate the symptoms associated with fibromyalgia.

Actionable Advice for Fibromyalgia and VNS

- **Consult with a healthcare provider:** Before considering VNS as a treatment option for fibromyalgia, it is important to consult with a healthcare provider who can assess your condition and determine if VNS is appropriate for you.

- **Explore non-invasive VNS devices:** There are non-invasive VNS devices available that can be used at home to stimulate the vagus nerve. These devices may provide a convenient and safe option for individuals seeking to incorporate VNS into their fibromyalgia management.

- **Combine VNS with other therapies:** VNS can be used in conjunction with other therapies such as medication, physical therapy, and lifestyle modifications to enhance the overall management of fibromyalgia symptoms.

VNS for Chronic Pain

Chronic pain is a complex condition that can have a profound impact on a person's quality of life. VNS has shown promise in providing relief for individuals suffering from chronic pain by modulating pain signals and reducing inflammation. By targeting the vagus nerve, VNS can help regulate the body's pain response and potentially alleviate chronic pain symptoms.

Actionable Advice for Chronic Pain and VNS

- **Consider VNS as an adjunct therapy:** Individuals with chronic pain may benefit from incorporating VNS as an adjunct therapy to their existing pain management plan. Consult with a healthcare provider to determine if VNS is a suitable option for your specific condition.

- **Practice self-care techniques:** In addition to VNS therapy, incorporating self-care techniques such as relaxation exercises, mindfulness, and gentle physical activity can help manage chronic pain and improve overall well-being.

- **Monitor and track progress:** Keep track of your symptoms and pain levels while undergoing VNS therapy to assess its effectiveness in managing chronic pain. Share this information with your healthcare provider for personalized care.

VNS for Autoimmune Diseases

Autoimmune diseases are characterized by the body's immune system attacking its tissues, leading to inflammation and tissue damage. VNS has emerged as a potential treatment option for autoimmune diseases by modulating the immune response and reducing inflammation.

By targeting the vagus nerve, VNS may help regulate the immune system and alleviate symptoms associated with autoimmune diseases.

Actionable Advice for Autoimmune Diseases and VNS

- **Consult with a specialist:** If you have been diagnosed with an autoimmune disease and are considering VNS therapy, consult with a specialist in both neurology and immunology to determine the best course of treatment for your specific condition.

- **Adopt an anti-inflammatory diet:** In conjunction with VNS therapy, adopting an anti-inflammatory diet rich in fruits, vegetables, and omega-3 fatty acids may help manage the symptoms of autoimmune diseases and support overall health.

- **Prioritize stress management:** Chronic stress can exacerbate the symptoms of autoimmune diseases. Incorporate stress-reducing activities such as meditation, yoga, or deep breathing exercises to complement VNS therapy and support your immune system.

Overall, vagus nerve stimulation shows promise as a novel therapy for conditions such as fibromyalgia, chronic pain, and autoimmune diseases by modulating pain signals, inflammation, and the immune response. By understanding the potential benefits of VNS and incorporating actionable advice into your treatment plan, you can explore this innovative therapy as part of your journey towards improved health and well-being. Remember, always consult with a healthcare provider before starting any new treatment regimen to ensure it is safe and appropriate for your individual needs.

Chapter 7

Vagus Nerve Stimulation Techniques

We've given some advice for each particular issue so far, but in this chapter, let's really delve into how you can stimulate the vagus nerve and get the best out of the approach you're taking. It's all very well and good to tell you to go out and speak to people, be sociable, breathe deeply, and do some yoga, but how?

That's what we're going to answer in this chapter.

We're about to get practical, so buckle up!

Overview of Vagus Nerve Stimulation (VNS)

We touched up on Vagus Nerve Stimulation earlier, but let's delve right into the details.

Vagus nerve stimulation, also known as VNS, is a fascinating therapeutic approach that involves the use of a device to provide electrical stimulation to the vagus nerve, an essential part of the nervous system responsible for controlling many bodily functions. Let's dive into the intricate workings of this remarkable treatment method.

The vagus nerve is the longest cranial nerve in the body, running from the brainstem through the neck and branching out to various organs in the chest and abdomen. It plays a crucial role in regulating key bodily processes such as heart rate, digestion, and inflammation. By targeting this important nerve with electrical stimulation, VNS can modulate the communication between the brain and the body, leading to a range of potential therapeutic benefits.

So, how does vagus nerve stimulation work on a technical level? The process begins with the implantation of a small device – typically a generator – under the skin in the chest area. This generator is connected to a lead that is carefully placed around the vagus nerve, usually on the left side of the neck. Once in position, the device is programmed to deliver electrical impulses to the nerve at regular intervals determined by a healthcare provider.

These electrical impulses travel along the vagus nerve to the brainstem, where they influence the activity of various brain regions involved in regulating mood, behavior, and autonomic functions. By modulating the neural signals passing through the vagus nerve, VNS can have a profound impact on conditions such as epilepsy, depression, and chronic pain.

One of the key mechanisms by which vagus nerve stimulation exerts its effects is through the activation of the locus coeruleus, a brain region involved in the release of neurotransmitters such as norepinephrine. This activation can lead to changes in brain activity that help regulate mood and emotional responses, providing relief for individuals with depression or anxiety disorders.

In addition to its effects on the brain, VNS can also influence the activity of the autonomic nervous system, which controls involuntary functions such as heart rate and digestion. By modulating the parasympathetic branch of the autonomic nervous system, vagus nerve stimulation can help regulate heart rate variability, reduce inflammation, and improve overall well-being.

Interestingly, VNS has been shown to have anti-inflammatory effects, which may contribute to its therapeutic benefits in conditions such as rheumatoid arthritis and inflammatory bowel disease. By dampening the body's inflammatory response, VNS can help alleviate symptoms and improve the quality of life for individuals with these chronic conditions.

Another fascinating aspect of vagus nerve stimulation is its potential to enhance memory and cognitive function. Research has shown that VNS can improve learning and memory in both animal models and human studies, suggesting that this therapeutic approach may have applications in the treatment of cognitive disorders such as Alzheimer's disease.

Overall, vagus nerve stimulation offers a promising avenue for treating a variety of neurological and psychiatric conditions by harnessing the body's own neural pathways. By targeting the vagus nerve with controlled electrical impulses, this innovative therapy can modulate brain activity, regulate autonomic functions, and reduce inflammation, leading to improved health and well-being for individuals in need.

Non-invasive Techniques to Stimulate the Vagus Nerve

Stimulating the vagus nerve through non-invasive techniques can have profound effects on both physical and mental well-being. If a more invasive option doesn't call out to you, there are some non-invasive options to try. Let's explore various methods to stimulate the vagus nerve without the need for invasive procedures.

Deep Breathing Techniques

Deep breathing is a simple yet powerful way to stimulate the vagus nerve. By taking slow, deep breaths, you can activate the parasympathetic nervous system and promote relaxation.

Here are two exercises you can try:

Diaphragmatic Breathing

- Find a comfortable position, either sitting or lying down.
- Place one hand on your chest and the other on your abdomen.
- Inhale deeply through your nose, focusing on expanding your abdomen as you breathe in.
- Exhale slowly through your mouth, feeling your abdomen contract.
- Repeat this deep breathing pattern for a few minutes, focusing on the rise and fall of your diaphragm.

Alternate Nostril Breathing

- Sit comfortably with your spine straight.
- Place your left hand on your left knee, palm facing up.
- Use your right thumb to close off your right nostril, and inhale deeply through your left nostril.
- Close off your left nostril with your right ring finger and exhale through your right nostril.
- Keeping your left nostril closed, inhale through your right nostril.
- Close off your right nostril and exhale through your left nostril.

- Continue this alternate breathing pattern for several minutes, focusing on the rhythm of your breath and the sensation of air passing through each nostril.

These exercises can help activate the parasympathetic nervous system through deep, mindful breathing, which in turn can stimulate the vagus nerve and promote relaxation and overall well-being.

Cold Exposure

Exposing your body to cold temperatures, such as cold showers or swimming in cold water, can stimulate the vagus nerve. The shock of cold triggers the body's fight or flight response, leading to vagus nerve activation.

Cold Water Face Immersion Technique

- Fill a basin with cold water.
- Take a deep breath and submerge your face in the cold water for about 30 seconds to 1 minute.
- Focus on your breathing and try to remain calm while you feel the cold sensation on your face.
- After the time is up, slowly lift your face out of the water and take a few deep breaths.
- Repeat this exercise a few times, gradually increasing the duration of immersion.

Cold Shower Therapy

- Start by taking your regular warm shower.
- Gradually turn the water temperature to cold, starting from your feet and moving upwards to your head.
- Stay under the cold water for about 1-3 minutes while focusing on your breath and trying to relax.
- Feel the sensation of the cold water on your skin and try to embrace it rather than resist it.
- After the cold exposure, switch back to warm water to help your body gradually warm up.
- Practice this cold shower therapy regularly to help stimulate your vagus nerve and improve your overall well-being.

Meditation and Mindfulness

Practicing meditation and mindfulness can help calm the mind and stimulate the vagus nerve. Mindful breathing exercises and body scans can enhance vagal tone and promote relaxation. Dedicate 10-15 minutes each day to meditation or mindfulness practice. Focus on your breath, and sensations in your body, and bring awareness to the present moment.

Loving-Kindness Meditation

- Begin by finding a quiet and peaceful space to sit comfortably.
- Close your eyes and take a few deep breaths to center yourself.
- Repeat the following phrases silently or aloud:
    - "May I be happy?
    - May I be healthy?
    - May I be safe?
    - May I live with ease?"
- Visualize a sphere of warm, loving energy surrounding you as you send these wishes to yourself.
- Next, imagine someone you care about deeply (a loved one, friend, or pet) and direct the same phrases towards them.
- Extend this practice to include all beings, sending out feelings of compassion and kindness to everyone in the world.

This meditation helps stimulate the vagus nerve by fostering a sense of connection, empathy, and positivity, which are all beneficial for overall well-being.

Gratitude Meditation

- Find a quiet and comfortable space where you can sit or lie down in a relaxed position.
- Close your eyes and take a few deep breaths, inhaling slowly through your nose and exhaling through your mouth.
- Bring your attention to your breath. Notice the sensation of the air entering your nostrils, filling your lungs, and exhaling out.
- Now, shift your focus to your heart center. Visualize a warm, soothing light radiating from this area, spreading throughout your body.
- As you continue to breathe deeply and slowly, imagine sending gratitude and compassion to yourself and those around you.
- Now, gently place one hand on your chest and the other hand on your stomach. Feel the gentle rise and fall of your breath with each inhalation and exhalation.
- Next, bring your awareness to your throat and the area around it. Take a moment to swallow and notice the sensation in this area.
- Slowly begin to hum or chant a soothing sound, feeling the vibrations in your throat and chest. This gentle vocalization can help stimulate the vagus nerve.

- As you hum, visualize the vibrations traveling down your body, connecting with the vagus nerve and promoting relaxation and calmness.
- Take a few more deep breaths and then slowly open your eyes. Sit quietly for a moment, noticing how you feel after the meditation.

Singing and Chanting

Engaging in singing or chanting activities can stimulate the vagus nerve through the vibrations produced by vocal cords. Singing has been shown to increase heart rate variability, an indicator of vagal tone.

It can be as simple as singing along to your favorite songs, joining a choir or singing group, or practicing chanting mantras for a few minutes each day to stimulate the vagus nerve.

Humming Meditation

- Sit or stand comfortably with your back straight and relaxed.
- Take a few deep breaths to center yourself.
- Start humming, creating a soft, low-toned sound.
- Focus on the vibration in your chest and throat as you continue to hum.
- Imagine the sound traveling down your throat and vibrating through your body.

- Slowly increase the volume and intensity of your humming.
- Feel the vibration expanding throughout your body, resonating with your vagus nerve.
- Continue humming for a few minutes, allowing yourself to relax and let go of any tension.
- After a few minutes, gradually decrease the volume of your humming until it fades away.
- Take a moment to sit quietly and notice any changes in how you feel.

Vowel Chanting

- Find a comfortable seated position with your back straight and shoulders relaxed.
- Take a deep breath and exhale slowly to release any tension in your body.
- Begin chanting the vowel sounds: "A, E, I, O, U" in a continuous loop.
- Focus on each sound as it vibrates through your throat, chest, and abdomen.
- Feel the resonance of each vowel sound stimulating your vagus nerve.
- Experiment with varying the pitch and intensity of your chanting to find what feels most soothing.

- Allow the sounds to flow naturally, without forcing or straining.
- Continue chanting for a few minutes, allowing the vibrations to reverberate through your body.
- Gradually slow down the chanting until you come to a peaceful stop.
- Take a moment to sit in silence and notice any sensations or relaxation in your body and mind.

These exercises are designed to help you connect with and stimulate your vagus nerve through the power of sound and vibration.

Laughter Therapy

Laughter is a natural way to stimulate the vagus nerve and promote relaxation. The act of laughing triggers the release of endorphins and activates the parasympathetic nervous system.

It's simple too. Just incorporate laughter into your daily routine by watching comedies, sharing jokes with friends, or engaging in laughter yoga sessions. Or you can try these fun exercises:

Funny Faces

Have the participants make exaggerated and silly facial expressions for a minute or two. Encourage them to really go for it and make the most ridiculous faces they can think of. This exercise not only promotes laughter but also stimulates the muscles in the face, which can in turn stimulate the vagus nerve.

Story Time Laughter

Have the group sit in a circle and start telling a story, but with a twist - every time a certain word is mentioned (e.g. "banana"), everyone has to burst into laughter, no matter what. This unexpected laughter can activate the vagus nerve and help to create a fun and positive atmosphere. Rotate the word throughout the story to keep the laughter going.

Acupuncture

Acupuncture is an ancient Chinese medical practice that involves inserting thin needles into specific points on the body to promote healing and balance. According to traditional Chinese medicine (TCM) principles, acupuncture helps restore the flow of Qi (pronounced "chee"), the vital energy that flows through the body along meridian pathways.

From a modern perspective, acupuncture has gained popularity as a complementary therapy for managing various health conditions, including pain, anxiety, and digestion issues. The mechanism of action behind acupuncture's effectiveness is still a topic of research, but several theories have emerged to explain its benefits.

One of the proposed mechanisms of acupuncture is its ability to stimulate the release of endorphins, the body's natural painkillers. When the needles are inserted into specific acupuncture points, they trigger the release of endorphins, serotonin, and other neurotransmitters that help alleviate pain and improve mood.

Another theory suggests that acupuncture may modulate the body's nervous system, specifically the autonomic nervous system (ANS). The ANS comprises the sympathetic nervous system (fight or flight response) and the parasympathetic nervous system (rest and digest response). By stimulating certain acupuncture points, acupuncturists can help rebalance the ANS, promoting relaxation and stress reduction.

Now, let's dive into how acupuncture can help stimulate the vagus nerve.

Several acupuncture points along the body's meridians are believed to influence the vagus nerve indirectly. By targeting these points, acupuncturists can help regulate the activity of the vagus nerve, promoting a state of relaxation and reducing inflammation.

One of the key ways acupuncture stimulates the vagus nerve is through the activation of sensory fibers in the skin. When the acupuncture needles are inserted into specific points, they send signals to the brain, triggering a cascade of responses that ultimately lead to vagus nerve activation.

Research has shown that acupuncture can enhance vagal tone, which refers to the activity of the vagus nerve. Improved vagal tone is associated with better heart rate variability, indicating a healthier balance between the sympathetic and parasympathetic branches of the autonomic nervous system.

In addition to enhancing vagal tone, acupuncture has been found to reduce inflammation in the body. Chronic inflammation is linked to a range of health conditions, including autoimmune disorders, cardiovascular disease, and Alzheimer's disease. By stimulating the vagus nerve, acupuncture can help dampen the inflammatory response, promoting overall health and well-being.

Furthermore, acupuncture has been shown to promote the release of neurotransmitters like acetylcholine, which plays a key role in vagus nerve function. Acetylcholine is a neurotransmitter that helps regulate heart rate, digestion, and other autonomic functions. By boosting acetylcholine levels, acupuncture can support vagus nerve activity and improve overall nervous system function.

Overall, acupuncture offers a holistic approach to health and wellness by addressing the body's natural healing mechanisms. By stimulating the vagus nerve and modulating the autonomic nervous system, acupuncture can help improve various health conditions and promote a state of balance and well-being.

Medical Devices and Surgical Options

In recent years, there has been growing interest in the use of medical devices and surgical options to specifically target and enhance the function of the vagus nerve. While these shouldn't be your first port of call, let's talk about them to give you a fully-rounded impression of the vagus nerve and what you can do to simulate it.

Medical Devices for Vagus Nerve Stimulation

Vagus Nerve Stimulation (VNS) Therapy

We've already talked about this popular type of therapy, but let's sum it up here as it fits into this section very nicely.

Vagus Nerve Stimulation (VNS) therapy is a well-established treatment method for epilepsy and depression. It involves the implantation of a small device that delivers electrical impulses to the vagus nerve, helping to regulate abnormal brain activity and neurotransmitter levels. VNS therapy has been shown to be effective in reducing seizure frequency in epilepsy patients and improving mood in patients with treatment-resistant depression.

Transcutaneous Vagus Nerve Stimulation (tVNS)

Transcutaneous Vagus Nerve Stimulation (tVNS) is a non-invasive form of vagus nerve stimulation that involves applying electrical stimulation to the skin overlying the vagus nerve.

This method is used to modulate autonomic nervous system activity and has shown promise in treating conditions such as chronic pain, depression, and anxiety. tVNS devices are portable and can be used at home, making them a convenient option for patients seeking ongoing vagus nerve stimulation therapy.

Auricular Vagus Nerve Stimulation (aVNS)

Auricular Vagus Nerve Stimulation (aVNS) involves stimulating the vagus nerve through the ear using specialized devices. By targeting specific areas of the ear that are connected to the vagus nerve, aVNS can modulate autonomic nervous system function and promote relaxation and stress reduction.

This form of vagus nerve stimulation has been studied for its potential benefits in treating conditions such as PTSD, insomnia, and inflammatory disorders.

Implantable Vagus Nerve Stimulation Devices

Implantable vagus nerve stimulation devices are surgically implanted under the skin and provide continuous electrical stimulation to the vagus nerve. These devices are typically used in the treatment of epilepsy, depression, and chronic pain.

Implantable VNS devices have adjustable settings that allow healthcare providers to tailor the stimulation parameters to each individual patient's needs.

Surgical Options for Vagus Nerve Stimulation

Vagus Nerve Decompression

Vagus nerve decompression is a surgical procedure that involves relieving compression or irritation of the vagus nerve. This can be caused by surrounding structures, such as blood vessels or tumors, putting pressure on the nerve.

By decompressing the vagus nerve, surgeons can alleviate symptoms such as chronic cough, voice hoarseness, and swallowing difficulties.

Vagus Nerve Truncation

Vagus nerve truncation is a surgical procedure that involves cutting a portion of the vagus nerve to disrupt abnormal signaling patterns. This method is sometimes used in the treatment of severe cases of epilepsy or treatment-resistant depression where other therapies have been ineffective.

Vagus nerve truncation is a last-resort option and is only considered when all other treatment options have been exhausted.

Vagus Nerve Stimulation for Obesity

In recent years, vagus nerve stimulation has been explored as a potential treatment for obesity. Surgical options such as laparoscopic implantation of vagus nerve stimulators have been studied for their ability to reduce appetite and promote weight loss. These devices deliver electrical impulses to the vagus nerve, leading to decreased food intake and improved metabolism.

While still considered experimental, vagus nerve stimulation for obesity shows promise as a novel approach to combating this widespread health issue.

Vagus Nerve Stimulation for Inflammatory Disorders

Vagus nerve stimulation has also shown potential as a treatment for inflammatory disorders such as rheumatoid arthritis and inflammatory bowel disease. By modulating the activity of the vagus nerve, researchers believe that it may be possible to dampen the body's inflammatory response and reduce symptoms of these chronic conditions.

Surgical options for vagus nerve stimulation in inflammatory disorders are still in the early stages of research but hold promise for the future of immune-modulating therapies.

Medical devices and surgical options for stimulating and improving vagus nerve function offer a range of innovative approaches to treating a variety of health conditions. From vagus nerve stimulation therapy for epilepsy and depression to surgical interventions for obesity and inflammatory disorders, there are numerous possibilities for harnessing the power of the vagus nerve to enhance overall well-being.

As research continues to advance in this field, the development of more targeted and effective treatments for vagus nerve dysfunction holds promise for improving the quality of life for many patients in the future.

Chapter 8

The Mind-Body Connection

The mind-body connection is a fascinating and complex relationship. Let's dig deeper.

Our minds and bodies are not separate entities, but rather intricately intertwined, working in harmony to shape our experiences and perceptions of the world around us. The mind-body connection is a powerful force that influences every aspect of our lives, from our thoughts and emotions to our physical health and vitality.

As we delve deeper into the complexities of this connection, we begin to unravel the mysteries of how our thoughts and feelings can impact our physical health, and vice versa. The mind has the remarkable ability to influence the body's response to stress, leading to a cascade of physiological changes that can either enhance or detract from our well-being.

Chronic stress has been shown to have a profound impact on both our mental and physical health, leading to a host of conditions ranging from anxiety and depression to heart disease and chronic pain. By understanding how stress affects the body on a biological level, we can begin to take proactive steps to reduce its impact and promote overall well-being.

Exploring the mind-body connection also opens up a world of possibilities for enhancing our health and happiness through practices such as mindfulness, meditation, and yoga. These ancient practices have been shown to have profound effects on both the mind and body, promoting relaxation, stress reduction, and overall well-being.

In delving into the mind-body connection, we also explore the fascinating field of psychoneuroimmunology, which examines the intricate interplay between the mind, the nervous system, and the immune system. This emerging field of study sheds light on how our thoughts and emotions can influence our immune response, highlighting the powerful role that our mental state plays in shaping our physical health.

How the Vagus Nerve Mediates the Mind-Body Connection

The vagus nerve plays a crucial role in the parasympathetic nervous system, which is responsible for regulating many bodily functions at rest and during relaxation. But what makes the vagus nerve truly intriguing is its ability to bridge the gap between the mind and body, orchestrating a complex network of communication that influences our overall well-being.

One of the key ways in which the vagus nerve impacts the mind-body connection is through its role in the body's stress response. When we experience stress, whether it be physical or emotional, the sympathetic nervous system is activated, leading to the familiar "fight or flight" response. However, the vagus nerve acts as a counterbalance to this stress response by initiating the body's relaxation response through its parasympathetic function. This helps bring our bodies back to a state of equilibrium after the stress has passed, promoting relaxation and reducing the impact of chronic stress on our health.

Furthermore, the vagus nerve is intricately linked to our emotional well-being. Research has shown that the vagus nerve plays a significant role in regulating our mood and emotional responses. When the vagus nerve is functioning optimally, it can help modulate our emotions, promote feelings of calmness, and increase our resilience to emotional challenges. This connection between the vagus nerve and our emotional state highlights the important role it plays in the mind-body relationship.

Moreover, the vagus nerve is also involved in the gut-brain axis, the bidirectional communication pathway between the gut and the brain. As it innervates many of the organs in the abdomen, including the stomach and intestines, the vagus nerve plays a crucial role in regulating digestion and influencing our gut health. Interestingly, emerging research suggests that the health of the gut microbiome, which is the community of microorganisms living in our digestive system, can impact the function of the vagus nerve and, in turn, influence our mood and cognitive function. This further underscores the intricate interplay between the vagus nerve, our gut health, and our overall well-being.

In addition to its role in stress regulation, emotional well-being, and gut health, the vagus nerve is also involved in promoting restorative sleep. Adequate sleep is essential for our physical and mental health, and the vagus nerve contributes to the regulation of our sleep-wake cycle. By promoting relaxation and reducing stress, the vagus nerve helps prepare our bodies for restful sleep, allowing us to recharge and rejuvenate both our mind and body.

There's more! The vagus nerve has been implicated in the body's inflammatory response. Inflammation is a natural process that helps the body fight off infections and heal from injuries. However, chronic inflammation has been linked to a variety of health issues, including autoimmune diseases, heart disease, and mood disorders. The vagus nerve plays a crucial role in regulating inflammation by communicating with the immune system and exerting anti-inflammatory effects. This connection highlights the vital role of the vagus nerve in maintaining a balanced immune response and protecting our overall health.

So, as we can see, the vagus nerve serves as a vital link between the mind and body, orchestrating a symphony of communication that influences our overall health and well-being. From regulating our stress response and emotional state to promoting gut health and restorative sleep, the vagus nerve plays a multifaceted role in maintaining the delicate balance between mind and body.

Practice to Enhance Vagal Tone

We've covered a few practices to help stimulate the vagus nerve, but what about affecting your vagal tone in general? Some of this overlaps, but there are many different exercises you can try within each practice. So, if you've heard some in the last section, let's give you even more exercises that can focus on vagal tone in particular and not just general stimulation.

The key thing to remember is that you need to practice these regularly. The more you practice, the more effect you'll have on your vagal tone over the long term.

First, remember that enhancing vagal tone is like giving your body's natural relaxation system a tune-up. A healthy vagus nerve promotes better digestion, reduced inflammation, lower stress levels, improved mood, and overall well-being.

Here are some practices to help boost your vagal tone:

Deep Breathing for Vagal Tone

We know that slow, deep breathing stimulates the vagus nerve and activates the relaxation response. Here are two advanced deep breathing techniques that focus on improving vagal tone in particular.

Resonant Frequency Breathing

This technique involves finding your individual resonant breathing frequency, which is typically around 5-7 breaths per minute.

- Sit or lie down comfortably, and take slow, deep breaths in and out through the nose.
- Gradually decrease the length of each breath cycle while maintaining a smooth and even rhythm.

- Use a timer or a breathing app to help maintain consistency and gradually increase the duration of the practice over time.

Resonant-frequency breathing has been shown to increase heart rate variability and improve vagal tone.

Extended Exhalation Breathing

This technique involves extending the exhale phase of your breathing cycle to stimulate the parasympathetic nervous system and enhance vagal tone.

- Start by inhaling deeply and slowly through the nose for a count of 4, then exhale even more slowly and completely through the mouth for a count of 8.
- Focus on completely emptying the lungs and engaging the diaphragm to push out every last bit of air.
- Repeat this pattern for several minutes, gradually increasing the length of the exhalation as you become more comfortable with the practice.

Extended-exhalation breathing can help reduce stress and anxiety while promoting relaxation and vagal tone improvement.

Yoga and Tai Chi

These mind-body practices promote relaxation, mindfulness, and gentle movement, all of which can stimulate the vagus nerve.

Here are four particularly useful yoga poses, followed by two Tai Chi exercises.

Bridge Pose (Setu Bandhasana)

This pose helps stimulate the vagus nerve by opening the chest and throat area, which can help regulate heart rate and blood pressure.

To do the bridge pose, also known as Setu Bandhasana in yoga, you can follow these steps:

- Lie on your back with your knees bent and your feet flat on the floor, hip-width apart.
- Press your feet into the floor as you lift your hips up toward the ceiling.
- Interlace your fingers underneath your back and press your arms into the ground for support.
- Make sure your thighs are parallel to each other and your knees are directly above your ankles.
- Keep your neck and head relaxed on the mat.
- Hold the pose for a few breaths, then slowly lower your hips back down to the starting position.

Supported Shoulderstand (Salamba Sarvangasana)

This inversion pose can improve vagal tone by promoting relaxation and reducing stress. It also helps to calm the nervous system and improve circulation.

Here's a step-by-step guide on how to do the supported Shoulderstand pose:

- Start by laying down on your back with your arms by your sides, palms facing down.
- Bend your knees and bring your feet up towards your buttocks.
- Press your hands into the floor and lift your legs up towards the ceiling, using your core strength.
- Continue to lift your legs until they are perpendicular to the floor.
- Support your lower back with your hands, keeping your elbows close to your body.
- Slowly walk your hands down your back towards your shoulder blades, lifting your hips higher as you do so.
- Find a comfortable position with your hands supporting your lower back and your legs extended straight up towards the ceiling.
- Keep your neck and head in a neutral position, with your gaze towards your toes.

- Hold the pose for 5–10 breaths, breathing deeply and maintaining a steady foundation with your hands supporting your back.
- To come out of the pose, slowly release your hands from your back and gently roll down one vertebra at a time until your legs are back on the floor.

Legs Up the Wall Pose (Viparita Karani)

This gentle inversion pose can help stimulate the vagus nerve and improve circulation. It also promotes relaxation and reduces anxiety, which can have a positive impact on vagal tone.

Here's how to do the pose:

- Find a clear wall space: Locate a wall with enough space for you to lie down comfortably with your legs extended.
- Sit close to the wall: Sit sideways next to the wall with your hip touching it.
- Lie down on your back: Slowly lower your back to the ground while extending your legs up the wall. Your hips should be touching the wall, and your legs should be straight up.
- Adjust your position: Scoot your hips closer to the wall if you need to until you feel comfortable. Your body should be in an L-shape, with your legs supported by the wall and your torso resting on the ground.

- Relax and breathe: Close your eyes, relax your arms by your sides, and focus on your breath. Stay in this pose for 5–15 minutes, breathing deeply and allowing your body to relax.
- Release the pose: To come out of the pose, gently bend your knees towards your chest, roll onto one side, and slowly sit up.

Reclining Bound Angle Pose (Supta Baddha Konasana)

This restorative pose opens the chest and abdomen, helping to stimulate the vagus nerve. It also promotes relaxation and deep breathing, which can improve vagal tone and overall well-being.

Here is how you can do the Reclining Bound Angle Pose (Supta Baddha Konasana):

- Begin by sitting on the floor with your legs extended in front of you.
- Bend your knees and bring the soles of your feet together, letting your knees fall out to the sides.
- Slowly lean back, supporting yourself with your hands as you lower your back to the floor. You can use a pillow or yoga block under your back for support if needed.
- Allow your arms to relax by your sides, palms facing up.

- Close your eyes and focus on your breath, allowing your body to relax and sink deeper into the pose.
- Stay in this pose for 5–10 minutes, breathing deeply and feeling the opening in your hips and groin area.
- When you are ready to come out of the pose, gently bring your knees together and roll to one side before slowly coming up to a seated position.

Remember to listen to your body and only go as far into the pose as feels comfortable for you.

Here are two Tai Chi exercises that can help improve vagal tone:

Breathing Exercise with Tai Chi Movement

- Start by standing in a relaxed posture with your feet shoulder-width apart and your knees slightly bent.
- Take a few deep breaths to center yourself.
- Begin a simple Tai Chi movement, such as "Cloud Hands."
- Keep your back straight, shoulders relaxed, and arms at your sides.
- Begin by shifting your weight to your right leg while simultaneously turning your upper body to the right.
- Lift your left hand up to shoulder height with your palm facing down, and extend your right hand downwards with your palm facing up.

- Slowly shift your weight to your left leg as you bring your right hand up to shoulder height with your palm facing down and extend your left hand downwards with your palm facing up. Your body should now be facing the left side.
- Continue this fluid motion of shifting your weight from side to side while moving your hands in a circular motion. Imagine that you are gently pushing clouds away as you move gracefully from one side to the other.
- As you practice, focus on your breathing and try to synchronize your movements with each inhale and exhale. Remember to keep your movements smooth and controlled, maintaining a sense of calm and relaxation throughout.
- Repeat the Cloud Hands movement for several minutes, allowing your body to flow naturally with the gentle rhythm of the exercise.

Meditative Standing Exercise

- Stand in a comfortable and stable position with your feet rooted to the ground.
- Close your eyes and focus on your breath, allowing it to become slow and deep.
- Imagine a sense of calm and relaxation spreading throughout your body as you continue breathing deeply.

- Engage in gentle swaying or rocking movements, mimicking the flow of energy within your body.

This meditative standing practice can help activate the vagus nerve and promote a state of relaxation and well-being.

Meditation

Mindfulness meditation has been shown to increase vagal tone. Take a few minutes each day to sit quietly, focus on your breath, and cultivate a sense of calm and awareness. This can have a profound impact on your vagal tone over time.

Here are two advanced meditation techniques that are ideal for vagal tone improvement.

Humming Meditation

- Sit comfortably in a quiet space.
- Close your eyes and take a few deep breaths to center yourself. Begin to lightly hum a simple, soothing melody.
- Focus on the vibration of the humming in your throat and chest.
- As you continue to hum, bring your awareness to the sensations in your body and any emotions that may arise.

- The vibrations from the humming can help stimulate the vagus nerve, which in turn can enhance the vagal tone.
- Practice this meditation for at least 10–15 minutes daily for optimal benefits.

Gut-Brain Connection Meditation

- Find a quiet and comfortable place to sit or lie down.
- Close your eyes and bring your awareness to your gut area.
- Visualize a warm, healing light radiating from your gut and spreading throughout your body.
- As you focus on this light, imagine it communicating with your brain, establishing a harmonious connection between your gut and brain.

This visualization practice can help enhance the communication between the gut and brain, which is closely tied to the vagus nerve and can positively impact the vagal tone. Practice this meditation regularly to strengthen the gut-brain connection and improve overall well-being.

Cold Exposure

We know that cold showers or immersion in cold water can activate the vagus nerve, but advanced techniques done regularly can increase vagal tone. Start slowly and build up your tolerance over time. Even splashing cold water on your face can have a similar effect.

Ice Pack on the Neck

Place a cold ice pack on the back of your neck for 3-5 minutes. The vagus nerve runs close to the surface in this area, and the cold temperature can help stimulate and tone the nerve.

Immersion in Cold Water

If you have access to a cold body of water, like a pool or natural body of water, consider immersing yourself for a short period of time. Start with shorter durations and gradually increase as your body adjusts. The cold water immersion can trigger the body's "dive reflex," activating the vagus nerve and improving its tone.

Remember to start slowly and gradually build up your tolerance to cold exposure exercises to avoid any negative effects. Over time, these exercises can help improve vagal tone and contribute to overall health and well-being.

Heart Rate Variability Biofeedback

This technique involves monitoring your heart rate variability, which is influenced by your vagal tone. By practicing coherence techniques through biofeedback devices, you can train your body to regulate stress responses and improve vagal tone.

Heart Rate Variability (HRV) is a measure of the variation in time intervals between heartbeats, reflecting the dynamic interplay between the sympathetic (fight-or-flight) and parasympathetic (rest-and-digest) branches of the autonomic nervous system. A high HRV indicates a healthy autonomic nervous system, adaptive stress response, and better overall health, whereas a low HRV may be indicative of stress, poor health, or decreased vagal tone.

So, how does it work?

HRV biofeedback involves monitoring and controlling heart rate variability patterns through real-time feedback mechanisms. By using specialized biofeedback devices or apps that measure HRV, individuals can learn to regulate their breathing and heart rate to improve vagal tone and achieve a state of coherence characterized by synchronized physiological rhythms and enhanced well-being.

Practicing HRV Biofeedback

- Find a quiet and comfortable place to sit or lie down.
- Begin by focusing on your breath, taking slow and deep breaths in through your nose and out through your mouth.
- Use a biofeedback device or app to monitor your heart rate variability in real-time.

- Adjust your breathing pattern to increase the variability between heartbeats, aiming for a smooth and coherent rhythm.
- Visualize positive emotions or experiences to enhance the coherence of your heart rate variability patterns.
- Practice HRV biofeedback regularly for at least 10–20 minutes a day to improve vagal tone and overall well-being.

Intermittent Fasting

Intermittent fasting (IF) has gained immense popularity in recent years as a dietary strategy that involves cycling between periods of eating and fasting. This approach is not just about weight loss; it has been touted for its potential health benefits, including improving vagal tone.

Intermittent fasting is not a diet in the traditional sense but rather a pattern of eating that alternates between periods of eating and fasting. Unlike traditional diets that focus on what to eat, intermittent fasting is more about when to eat. It does not specify which foods to eat but emphasizes the timing of meals.

There are several different methods of intermittent fasting, with the most common ones being time-restricted feeding, alternate-day fasting, and the 5:2 diet.

- **Time-Restricted Feeding (TRF):** Time-restricted feeding involves limiting your daily eating window to a specific number of hours, typically between 6 to 8 hours. The remaining hours of the day are considered the fasting period. For example, if you choose an 8-hour eating window from 12 pm to 8 pm, you would fast for the remaining 16 hours.

- **Alternate-Day Fasting:** This method involves alternating between days of regular eating and days of fasting. On fasting days, individuals may consume very few calories or nothing at all, while on non-fasting days, they eat normally.

- **5:2 Diet:** The 5:2 diet involves eating normally for five days of the week and restricting calorie intake to around 500-600 calories on two non-consecutive days. This approach allows for flexibility in choosing the fasting days.

Each of these methods has its own benefits and challenges, and individuals may choose the one that best fits their lifestyle and preferences.

Improving Vagal Tone through Intermittent Fasting

Intermittent fasting has been shown to positively influence vagal tone through several mechanisms:

- **Reduced Inflammation:** Fasting has been found to reduce inflammation in the body, which can have a direct impact on vagal tone. Chronic inflammation can impair vagal function, so by decreasing inflammation through fasting, vagal tone can be improved.

- **Enhanced Autophagy:** Autophagy is a process in which the body breaks down and recycles damaged cells and proteins. Fasting promotes autophagy, which not only helps in cellular repair but also supports vagal tone by maintaining the health of nerve cells.

- **Improved Gut Health:** The gut-brain axis plays a significant role in vagal tone, as the vagus nerve communicates bidirectionally between the gut and the brain. Intermittent fasting has been shown to promote a healthy gut microbiome, which in turn can positively influence vagal tone.

- **Decreased Oxidative Stress:** Fasting induces a state of mild stress in the body, leading to the activation of various cellular repair mechanisms. By reducing oxidative stress, intermittent fasting can support overall nerve health, including vagal tone.

- **Better Blood Sugar Regulation:** Intermittent fasting can help regulate blood sugar levels by improving insulin sensitivity. Stable blood sugar levels are essential for maintaining vagal tone, as fluctuations in glucose levels can impact nerve function.

By incorporating intermittent fasting into your lifestyle, you may experience improvements in vagal tone, which can have a ripple effect on overall health and well-being.

Remember to consult with a healthcare provider or nutritionist before making any significant changes to your diet, especially if you have underlying health conditions.

Gargling

Believe it or not, gargling with warm salt water can also help improve vagal tone, which is essential for maintaining a healthy nervous system and overall well-being.

Here are two exercises you can do to improve vagal tone through gargling:

Salt Water Gargle

- Mix a teaspoon of salt in a glass of warm water.
- Take a sip of the solution and tilt your head back slightly.
- Gargle the water in your mouth for about 30 seconds before spitting it out.
- Repeat this a few times to stimulate the vagus nerve and promote relaxation.

Sing or Hum While Gargling

Another effective way to enhance vagal tone through gargling is to incorporate singing or humming. After doing a salt water gargle, try singing a simple tune or humming a melody while keeping the water in your mouth. The vibrations created by vocalization, combined with the act of gargling, can further stimulate the vagus nerve.

Remember, consistency is key when it comes to enhancing vagal tone. Incorporate these practices into your daily routine, listen to your body, and be patient with yourself as you work towards improving your overall well-being through increased vagal tone. Your body and mind will thank you for it!

The Importance of Emotional and Psychological Health

Emotional and psychological health are essential components of overall well-being. All too often, we focus simply on physical health, but these elements are just as vital. After all, they are the pillars upon which we build our resilience, cope with challenges, and navigate life's ups and downs.

Let's dig a bit deeper to understand the profound significance of emotional and psychological health and explore why nurturing these aspects of ourselves is crucial for a fulfilling and balanced life.

To start, let's consider the interconnected nature of emotional and psychological health. Emotional health pertains to our ability to recognize, express, and manage our feelings in a healthy way. It involves being self-aware, understanding our emotions, and effectively coping with stress. On the other hand, psychological health encompasses our cognitive and emotional well-being, including our thoughts, beliefs, and attitudes. It involves finding meaning in life, building healthy relationships, and maintaining a positive outlook.

Together, emotional and psychological health shape our mental resilience and influence how we perceive and interact with the world around us. When these aspects are nurtured and prioritized, we are better equipped to handle life's challenges, bounce back from setbacks, and cultivate a sense of inner peace.

It is important to recognize the impact of emotional and psychological health on our physical well-being. Research has shown that chronic stress, anxiety, and other negative emotions can contribute to a range of physical health issues, such as cardiovascular disease, a weakened immune system, and digestive problems. By taking care of our emotional and psychological well-being, we can reduce the risk of developing such health issues and promote overall wellness.

Moreover, emotional and psychological health plays a significant role in our relationships with others. When we are in tune with our emotions and have a strong sense of self-awareness, we are better able to communicate effectively, empathize with others, and establish healthy boundaries. This, in turn, fosters deeper connections, enhances interpersonal relationships, and promotes a sense of belonging and community.

Cultivating emotional and psychological health also leads to improved decision-making and problem-solving abilities. When we are emotionally balanced and mentally clear, we are better equipped to think rationally, consider different perspectives, and make sound choices. This not only benefits our personal lives but also our professional endeavors, as we become more effective leaders, collaborators, and innovators.

One of the key aspects of nurturing emotional and psychological health is practicing self-care. This involves engaging in activities that promote relaxation, self-reflection, and emotional release. Whether it's meditating, journaling, exercising, or spending time in nature, taking time for oneself is crucial for maintaining a healthy emotional and psychological state.

Another essential component of emotional and psychological health is seeking support when needed. It's important to remember that asking for help is a sign of strength, not weakness. Whether it's talking to a trusted friend, seeking guidance from a therapist, or joining a support group, reaching out to others can provide valuable insight, perspective, and comfort during challenging times.

In addition to self-care and seeking support, developing emotional intelligence is paramount for nurturing emotional and psychological health. Emotional intelligence involves recognizing, understanding, and managing our own emotions, as well as being attuned to the emotions of others. By honing our emotional intelligence skills, we can enhance our self-awareness, interpersonal relationships, and overall well-being.

Furthermore, practicing mindfulness is a powerful tool for promoting emotional and psychological health. Mindfulness involves being present at the moment without judgment or distraction and observing one's thoughts and feelings with awareness. By incorporating mindfulness practices into our daily routines, such as mindful breathing, meditation, or body scans, we can cultivate a sense of calm, clarity, and inner peace.

If you're feeling like your emotional or psychological health is taking a hit, it's important to take action and seek support. Remember, it's absolutely okay not to be okay sometimes. Working on your vagal tone is one thing to do, but here are some other steps you can take.

You'll find that a lot of them overlap with vagal nerve stimulation, which shows just how easy this practice is to incorporate into your daily life.

- **Reach out to someone:** Whether it's a friend, family member, or mental health professional, sharing how you're feeling can be incredibly relieving.
- **Practice self-care:** Allocate time for activities that bring you joy and relaxation. This could be anything from going for a walk in nature, reading a book, or treating yourself to a nice meal.
- **Get moving:** Exercise is a wonderful way of boosting your mood and clearing your mind. Even a short walk or some gentle stretching can make a difference.
- **Explore mindfulness techniques:** Meditation, deep breathing exercises, or even just taking a moment to focus on the present can help calm your racing thoughts.
- **Consider professional help:** If you find that your emotional struggles persist, seek out a therapist or counselor who can provide invaluable support and guidance.

Remember, it's okay to not have all the answers right away. Allow yourself the time and space to navigate your emotions and be kind to yourself along the way. You're not alone in this journey towards better emotional well-being.

Chapter 9

Diet, Nutrition, and the Vagus Nerve

Imagine the vagus nerve as a superhighway of communication between the gut and the brain, influencing everything from digestion to mood. But did you know that the foods we consume can actually influence the health and activity of this vital nerve? It's like giving your vagus nerve a daily dose of nourishment and care through the foods on your plate.

Throughout this chapter, we will explore the impact of various nutrients, vitamins, and dietary choices on optimizing vagus nerve function. From probiotic-rich foods that promote gut health to anti-inflammatory nutrients that calm the nervous system, we'll uncover the keys to supporting a healthy vagal tone through mindful eating habits.

Get ready to empower yourself with practical insights and tips that can enhance both your physical well-being and mental health. It's time to feed your brain and gut with knowledge that nourishes from within.

The Impact of Diet on Vagal Tone

One of the factors that can influence vagal tone is diet. The foods we eat can either support or hinder the function of the vagus nerve, ultimately affecting our overall well-being. By making conscious choices about what we put into our bodies, we can positively impact our vagal tone and promote better health.

A Good Diet and Vagal Tone

A nutrient-dense diet rich in fruits, vegetables, whole grains, lean proteins, and healthy fats can have a positive impact on vagal tone. These foods provide essential nutrients that support the health of the vagus nerve and the parasympathetic nervous system. Here are some key components of a good diet that can help improve vagal tone:

- **Omega-3 Fatty Acids:** Foods rich in omega-3 fatty acids, such as fatty fish (salmon, mackerel, and sardines), flaxseeds, chia seeds, and walnuts, have anti-inflammatory properties that support vagal tone. Omega-3 fatty acids have been shown to reduce inflammation and improve heart rate variability, which is a marker of vagal tone.

- **Fiber-Rich Foods:** Fiber is essential for gut health, and a healthy gut is crucial for optimal vagal tone. Foods high in fiber, such as fruits, vegetables, legumes, and whole grains, support the growth of beneficial gut bacteria, which play a role in regulating the parasympathetic nervous system.

- **Antioxidant-Rich Foods:** Antioxidants help protect cells from damage caused by free radicals and oxidative stress, which can impact vagal tone. Foods like berries, dark leafy greens, nuts, seeds, and green tea are rich in antioxidants and can support overall nerve health.

- **Probiotic-Rich Foods:** Probiotics are beneficial bacteria that support gut health and play a role in regulating the vagus nerve. Fermented foods like yogurt, kefir, kimchi, sauerkraut, and kombucha can help maintain a healthy balance of gut bacteria and support vagal tone.

- **Balanced Macronutrients:** A diet that includes a balance of carbohydrates, proteins, and fats provides the body with the energy and nutrients it needs to function optimally. Maintaining stable blood sugar levels through balanced meals can help support vagal tone and overall nervous system health.

- **Adequate Hydration:** Staying hydrated is essential for overall health, including optimal nervous system function. Dehydration can affect nerve signaling, including the vagus nerve. Drinking an adequate amount of water throughout the day can support a healthy vagal tone.

Incorporating these dietary components into your daily eating habits can help support a healthy vagal tone and overall well-being. Remember, a good diet is not just about what you eat but also how you eat. Eating mindfully, chewing your food thoroughly, and enjoying meals in a relaxed environment can further support optimal vagal tone.

A Bad Diet and Vagal Tone

On the flip side, a poor diet high in processed foods, refined sugars, unhealthy fats, and artificial additives can have a negative impact on vagal tone. These dietary factors can contribute to inflammation, oxidative stress, and gut dysbiosis, all of which can disrupt the functioning of the vagus nerve and the parasympathetic nervous system. Here's how a bad diet can affect vagal tone:

- **Inflammatory Foods:** Processed foods, sugary treats, refined grains, and unhealthy fats can promote inflammation in the body, including the nervous system. Chronic inflammation can impair vagal tone and disrupt the balance of the autonomic nervous system, leading to dysregulation of bodily functions.
- **Sugar and High-Glycemic Foods:** Consuming excessive amounts of sugar and high-glycemic foods can spike blood sugar levels, leading to insulin resistance and metabolic dysfunction. Poor blood sugar control can impact nerve health and vagal tone, affecting the body's ability to relax and recover.

- **Artificial Additives:** Artificial sweeteners, preservatives, colorings, and flavorings found in processed foods can have negative effects on gut health and overall nerve function. These additives may disrupt the gut microbiome, leading to dysbiosis and compromising vagal tone.

- **Lack of Nutrient-Dense Foods:** A diet lacking in essential nutrients like omega-3 fatty acids, antioxidants, vitamins, and minerals can deprive the body of the building blocks needed for optimal nerve function. Without proper nourishment, the vagus nerve may not function at its best, affecting the parasympathetic tone.

- **Excessive Caffeine and Alcohol:** While moderate consumption of caffeine and alcohol may not have significant negative effects on vagal tone, excessive intake can disrupt the balance of the autonomic nervous system. Both stimulants can interfere with sleep, stress levels, and overall nervous system function.

If your current diet includes a lot of processed foods, sugary snacks, and unhealthy fats, it may be beneficial to make gradual changes towards a more nutrient-dense, whole foods-based diet. By reducing your intake of inflammatory and processed foods and focusing on whole, natural foods, you can support your vagal tone and overall nervous system function.

Put simply, the connection between diet and vagal tone highlights the importance of nourishing your body with wholesome, nutrient-rich foods that support optimal nerve function. Remember, small changes in your eating habits can have a big impact on your health, so choose foods that support a healthy vagal tone and a balanced autonomic nervous system.

Good vs. Bad Eating Habits

It's not only about what you eat but also how you eat it. By adopting good eating habits and avoiding bad ones, we can positively influence our vagal tone and experience improved health and vitality.

Let's delve into some factors that can affect vagal tone through our eating habits:

Good Eating Habits

- **Mindful Eating:** One of the best habits you can cultivate is mindful eating. Being present and focused during meals can help signal to your body that it's time to rest and digest. Slow down, savor each bite, and pay attention to your body's hunger and fullness cues.
- **Balanced Meals:** Eating a well-balanced diet rich in nutrients is essential for supporting overall health, including vagal tone. Ensure your meals contain a good mix of protein, healthy fats, complex

carbohydrates, vitamins, and minerals to provide your body with the fuel it needs to function optimally.

- **Probiotic-Rich Foods:** Including probiotic-rich foods in your diet can benefit gut health, which is closely linked to vagal tone. Fermented foods like yogurt, kimchi, sauerkraut, and kefir can help maintain a healthy balance of gut bacteria, promoting a better vagal tone.

- **Hydration:** We've said it once; we'll say it again. Staying adequately hydrated is key for supporting your body's overall functioning, including the vagus nerve. Aim to drink plenty of water throughout the day to keep your body properly hydrated and maintain optimal vagal tone.

- **Regular Meal Times:** Establishing regular meal times can help regulate your body's internal clock and promote a sense of routine. Consistency in when you eat can support healthy digestion and signal to your body that it's time for nourishment and rest.

Bad Eating Habits

- **Overeating:** Consuming large portions of food in one sitting can put stress on your digestive system and may negatively impact your vagal tone. Overeating can lead to discomfort, bloating, and sluggishness, affecting the body's ability to efficiently process nutrients.

- **Excessive Caffeine:** While a moderate amount of caffeine can provide a temporary energy boost, consuming too much caffeine can overstimulate the nervous system and potentially affect vagal tone. Be mindful of your caffeine intake and consider opting for decaffeinated options or herbal teas.

- **Skipping Meals:** Irregular meal patterns, such as skipping meals or going for long periods without eating, can disrupt the body's natural rhythms and impact vagal tone. Consistent meal times signal to your body that it's time for nourishment and can support healthy digestion. However, there is some suggestion that intermittent fasting may actually help the vagus nerve. This is something you need to balance carefully and understand before you try it. Overall, regular meals are generally the better option.

- **High Sugar Intake:** Diets high in refined sugars and sugary beverages can lead to blood sugar spikes and crashes, affecting energy levels and potentially impacting vagal tone. Opt for natural sources of sweetness, like fruits, to satisfy your sweet tooth without compromising your health.

- **Eating Late at Night:** Consuming heavy meals late at night can disrupt your body's natural sleep-wake cycle and digestive processes. Late-night eating may lead to indigestion, reflux, and discomfort, potentially affecting your vagal tone and overall well-being.

By incorporating good eating habits and minimizing bad ones, you can support a healthy vagal tone and promote overall wellness. Remember that every small change you make towards a healthier diet and lifestyle can have a significant impact on your body's ability to function optimally. Stay mindful, stay balanced, and nourish yourself with foods that support your well-being.

How Crash Diets and Binge Eating Affect the Vagus Nerve

Yo-yo dieting, unsustainable dieting, crash dieting, and binge eating can have a significant impact on the vagus nerve, which plays a crucial role in regulating various bodily functions. Unfortunately, we live in a society that encourages us to follow diets and try to fit into a so-called "acceptable" body type.

Put simply, you should forget about all of that, but to help you, let's look at how these unhealthy eating patterns can negatively affect the vagus nerve and, consequently, overall well-being:

Yo-yo Dieting

Yo-yo dieting, also known as weight cycling, involves repeatedly losing and gaining weight through cycles of restrictive eating and subsequent overeating. This pattern of fluctuating weight can lead to chronic inflammation, which can impact the vagus nerve's function.

Inflammation in the body can disrupt communication between the brain and the gut, affecting satiety signals and potentially leading to dysregulation of appetite and metabolism.

Unsustainable Dieting

Unsustainable dieting practices, such as extreme calorie restriction or following fad diets that lack essential nutrients, can deprive the body of the fuel it needs to function optimally. Inadequate intake of nutrients can compromise the health of the vagus nerve, which relies on a balance of vitamins and minerals for proper functioning.

Nutrient deficiencies can impair neurotransmitter production and signal transmission along the vagus nerve, impacting digestion, heart rate, and mood regulation.

Crash Dieting

Crash diets, characterized by rapid and drastic weight loss achieved through severely reduced calorie intake, can trigger stress responses in the body. Stress activates the sympathetic nervous system, which counteracts the parasympathetic activities controlled by the vagus nerve.

Prolonged stress from crash dieting can lead to chronic dysregulation of the vagus nerve, disrupting digestive processes and contributing to symptoms like bloating, constipation, and acid reflux.

Binge Eating

Binge eating episodes involve consuming large quantities of food in a short period, often accompanied by feelings of guilt and loss of control. The rapid influx of calories and macronutrients during binge eating can overload the digestive system and trigger inflammation, which can impair vagus nerve function.

Chronic binge eating may disrupt the brain-gut axis, weakening the connection between the central nervous system and the gastrointestinal tract, leading to irregular appetite regulation and emotional eating patterns.

These detrimental effects on the vagus nerve can manifest in various symptoms, such as digestive issues (e.g., bloating, abdominal pain, constipation), irregular heart rate, mood disturbances, and disruptions in hunger cues and fullness signals. Long-term damage to the vagus nerve resulting from yo-yo dieting, unsustainable dieting, crash dieting, and binge eating can impact overall health and well-being.

It is essential to prioritize sustainable and balanced eating habits that nourish the body and support vagus nerve health. Incorporating nutrient-dense foods, practicing mindful eating, and establishing a healthy relationship with food can promote proper vagus nerve function and overall wellness. Remember, consistency and moderation are key to fostering a harmonious connection between the brain, gut, and vagus nerve.

Chapter 10

Lifestyle Changes for Vagus Nerve Health

In the fast-paced world we live in, prioritizing our health and well-being can often take a backseat to our busy schedules. But what if we told you that making a few simple lifestyle changes could have a significant impact on one of the key players in our body's nervous system - the vagus nerve?

While altering ingrained habits may not always be a walk in the park, rest assured that it is indeed possible with some mindful effort and dedication. In this chapter, we'll explore how taking steps to support and nurture your vagus nerve through lifestyle modifications can lead to profound benefits for your overall health and well-being.

Stress Management Techniques

Stress is an insidious force that can wreak havoc on both our mental and physical well-being, yet its effects are often underestimated or dismissed. From its detrimental impact on our immune system to its role in the development of chronic conditions like heart disease and diabetes, stress is a silent but potent adversary that demands our attention and understanding.

Why is stress bad for you? The answer lies in the intricate interplay between our minds and bodies. When we experience stress, our bodies kick into high gear, initiating the "fight or flight" response that has been essential for human survival throughout evolution. This response, orchestrated by the sympathetic nervous system, floods our bodies with adrenaline and cortisol, preparing us to confront or flee from perceived threats. While this response can be life-saving in short bursts, chronic stress leads to a perpetual state of activation that takes a toll on our health.

The mechanisms behind why stress is bad for us are manifold. Firstly, prolonged exposure to stress hormones like cortisol can impair the functioning of our immune system, making us more susceptible to infections and illnesses. Additionally, chronic stress can contribute to the development of inflammation throughout the body, a key driver of various diseases including arthritis, asthma, and even cancer.

Moreover, stress has a profound impact on our cardiovascular system, increasing the risk of hypertension, heart disease, and stroke. The constant barrage of stress hormones can elevate blood pressure, promote the buildup of plaque in the arteries, and disrupt the balance of cholesterol in our bloodstream. Over time, these changes can have grave consequences for our heart health and overall well-being.

But why does stress happen in the first place? Our modern lifestyles, with their relentless pace and pressures, can be a breeding ground for stress. Whether it's looming deadlines at work, financial worries, relationship conflicts, or health concerns, the sources of stress are endless and ubiquitous. Our brains, wired to detect and respond to threats, interpret these stressors as dangers to be dealt with, triggering the body's stress response.

Within the body, chronic stress sets off a cascade of physiological changes that can have far-reaching effects on our health. The hypothalamic-pituitary-adrenal (HPA) axis, a crucial component of our stress response system, becomes dysregulated with chronic stress. The hypothalamus in the brain signals the pituitary gland to release adrenocorticotropic hormone (ACTH), which in turn prompts the adrenal glands to release cortisol. These chronically elevated cortisol levels can disrupt various bodily functions, from immune regulation to metabolism.

One fascinating aspect of the stress response is the role of the vagus nerve, a key player in the body's parasympathetic nervous system. The vagus nerve plays a crucial role in regulating our body's relaxation response. When we are stressed, the vagus nerve can become compromised, leading to a reduced ability to counteract the activation of the sympathetic nervous system.

The vagus nerve is instrumental in modulating inflammation, with its branches reaching various organs, including the heart, lungs, and digestive system. When the vagus nerve is functioning optimally, it helps to keep inflammation in check and promotes a state of calm and balance in the body. However, chronic stress can dampen vagal tone, increasing the risk of inflammation and its associated health issues.

In addition to its role in inflammation, the vagus nerve is also involved in the regulation of heart rate, digestion, and mood. A strong vagal tone is associated with a slower heart rate, better digestion, and improved emotional resilience. By contrast, a weakened vagal tone resulting from chronic stress can lead to heart rhythm abnormalities, gastrointestinal disturbances, and an increased susceptibility to mood disorders like anxiety and depression.

That leads us nicely to how to manage stress.

Stress management is essential for maintaining our mental and physical well-being in today's fast-paced world. Here are some practical and proven strategies to help you combat stress:

Deep Breathing Exercises

One of the simplest yet most effective stress management techniques is deep breathing. By focusing on your breath and taking slow, deep breaths, you can activate your body's relaxation response, reducing anxiety and slowing down your heart rate.

We've already given you several deep breathing exercises throughout this book so far, and any of those will work to help you reduce stress. The key is consistency.

Progressive Muscle Relaxation

This technique involves tensing and then releasing each muscle group in your body, starting from your toes and working your way up to your head. By consciously relaxing your muscles, you can release physical tension and promote a sense of calmness.

Here's how to do it:

Progressive muscle relaxation is a wonderful technique to help reduce stress and promote relaxation in the body. Here is a step-by-step guide on how to do progressive muscle relaxation:

- Find a quiet and comfortable place to sit or lie down.

- Close your eyes and take a few deep breaths to relax your mind and body.
- Start by focusing on your feet. Tense the muscles in your toes and feet for about 5-10 seconds, then slowly release the tension and let your muscles relax. Pay attention to the sensation of relaxation in your feet.
- Move your focus to your calves and thighs. Tighten these muscles for 5-10 seconds, then release and feel the tension melting away.
- Continue this process, moving up your body. Tense and relax your stomach, chest, back, arms, shoulders, neck, and face, one by one.
- As you tense each muscle group, try to focus on the difference between tension and relaxation. Notice how different it feels when the muscles are relaxed.
- Remember to breathe deeply and slowly throughout the exercise.
- Once you have completed tensing and relaxing all your muscle groups, take a few moments to enjoy the overall feeling of relaxation in your body.
- Open your eyes when you are ready and take a moment to appreciate the sense of calmness and relaxation you have created.

Progressive muscle relaxation can be a very effective technique when practiced regularly. It can help you release physical tension, reduce stress levels, and improve overall well-being.

Mindfulness Meditation

We've talked about mindfulness and meditation separately, but when they come together, they work wonderfully to combat stress. Mindfulness meditation helps you stay present in the moment and become aware of your thoughts and feelings without judgment. By practicing mindfulness regularly, you can cultivate a greater sense of inner peace and reduce stress levels.

Here's an exercise to try:

Sure! Here is a simple walking mindfulness meditation exercise you can try:

- Find a quiet and peaceful place to walk where you won't be disturbed.
- Start by standing still and taking a few deep breaths to center yourself and bring your attention to the present moment.
- Begin walking slowly and mindfully, paying full attention to each step you take. Feel the sensation of your feet touching the ground, the muscles moving in your legs, and the rhythm of your breath.
- Notice the sights, sounds, and smells around you without getting caught up in them. Simply observe them as they come and go.

- If your mind starts to wander, gently bring your focus back to the physical sensations of walking. You can also use a simple mantra or affirmation to help anchor your attention, such as "I am present in this moment" or "I walk with awareness."
- Continue walking mindfully for as long as you like, allowing yourself to fully immerse in the experience of each step and being present in the moment.
- When you're ready to end the meditation, gradually slow down your pace and come to a stop. Take a moment to feel gratitude for this time you've given yourself to be mindful and present.

Physical Exercise

Engaging in regular physical exercise is not only beneficial for your physical health but also for your mental well-being. Exercise releases endorphins, the body's natural stress relievers, and helps you reduce anxiety and improve your mood.

You don't have to join the gym if that's not something that appeals to you. Going for a walk or a jog can be just as effective; even swimming does the trick. The key is making sure it's something you enjoy, while also doing it consistently.

Yoga

Yoga combines physical postures, breathing techniques, and meditation to help you achieve a sense of balance and relaxation. Practicing yoga regularly can help you improve flexibility, reduce muscle tension, and calm your mind.

Here is a great yoga routine for stress relief:

Of course! Here's a simple yoga routine that you can do to help relieve stress:

- Start in a seated position with your legs crossed. Take a few deep breaths to center yourself.
- **Begin with Cat-Cow pose:** Inhale as you arch your back and look up (Cow pose), then exhale as you round your back and tuck your chin to your chest (Cat pose). Repeat this flow for a few breaths.
- **Move into Child's pose:** Sit back on your heels, extend your arms forward, and rest your forehead on the mat. Hold this pose for a few breaths, focusing on releasing tension in your back and shoulders.
- **Transition into Downward Facing Dog:** Lift your hips up and back, pressing your hands and feet into the mat. Pedal your feet to stretch out the calves and hamstrings.
- **Flow through a few rounds of Sun Salutation:** Start in Mountain pose, then reach up to the sky in

Upward Salute, fold forward into Forward Fold, step back into Plank pose, lower down into Chaturanga, flow into Upward Facing Dog, and finally push back into Downward Facing Dog. Repeat this sequence a few times, moving with your breath.

- **End with Corpse pose:** Lie flat on your back, arms by your sides, palms facing up. Close your eyes and focus on deep, slow breaths. Stay in this pose for at least 5-10 minutes, allowing your body to fully relax.

Remember to listen to your body and modify any poses as needed.

Journaling

Writing down your thoughts and emotions can be a powerful way to process stress and gain perspective on challenging situations. Keeping a journal allows you to express yourself freely and identify patterns in your behavior that may be contributing to your stress.

Here are some tips for effective journaling:

- Set aside dedicated time for journaling each day. Consistency is key to reaping the benefits of stress relief through journaling.
- Find a quiet and comfortable space to write in where you can focus without distractions.

- Start by jotting down your thoughts and feelings uncensored. Don't worry about grammar or structure at first; just let your emotions flow onto the paper.
- Reflect on what triggers your stress and write about it. This can help you identify patterns and gain insights into what is causing your stress.
- Write down positive affirmations, gratitude lists, or things that bring you joy. Shifting your focus to positive thoughts can help reduce stress and improve your mood.
- Use journal prompts to spark inspiration and reflection. There are plenty of resources online with prompts specifically designed for stress relief.
- Consider incorporating mindfulness techniques into your journaling practice, such as deep breathing exercises or body scans, to help you stay present and grounded.
- Don't be too hard on yourself if you miss a day of journaling. Just pick up where you left off and continue to make it a habit.
- Experiment with different journaling formats, such as bullet journaling, art journaling, or gratitude journals, to find what works best for you.
- Remember, journaling is a personal practice, so allow yourself the freedom to explore and express yourself in a way that feels most comfortable and beneficial to you.

Healthy Eating

Eating a balanced diet rich in whole foods, fruits, and vegetables can support your body's ability to cope with stress. Avoiding excessive caffeine, sugar, and processed foods can help regulate your mood and energy levels.

Here are some foods you should pack into your daily diet for stress management:

- Berries such as blueberries, strawberries, and raspberries are rich in antioxidants that can help combat stress.
- Fatty fish like salmon, mackerel, and sardines are high in omega-3 fatty acids, which have been shown to reduce anxiety and stress.
- Nuts and seeds, such as almonds, walnuts, flaxseeds, and chia seeds, are good sources of healthy fats and magnesium, which can help reduce stress.
- Dark chocolate in moderation can help lower cortisol levels and reduce the effects of stress on the body.
- Green leafy vegetables like spinach, kale, and Swiss chard are high in magnesium, which can help relax the muscles and calm the nervous system.
- Whole grains such as quinoa, brown rice, and oats can help stabilize blood sugar levels and keep you feeling full and energized, reducing stress.

- Herbal teas like chamomile, peppermint, and lavender can have calming effects on the body and help reduce stress and anxiety.
- Avocados are packed with healthy fats and potassium, which can help lower blood pressure and reduce the effects of stress.
- Citrus fruits like oranges, lemons, and grapefruits are rich in vitamin C, which can help boost the immune system and combat stress.
- Fermented foods like yogurt, kefir, and sauerkraut contain probiotics that can support a healthy gut, which is linked to reduced stress and anxiety levels.

Incorporating these foods into your diet can help manage stress and improve your overall well-being.

Social Support

Connecting with friends, family, or support groups can provide a valuable outlet for sharing your feelings and receiving emotional support.

Talking to someone you trust about your stressors can help you feel understood and less alone.

Time Management

Effective time management can help you reduce stress by prioritizing tasks, setting realistic goals, and avoiding procrastination. Creating a daily or weekly schedule can help you stay organized and in control of your responsibilities.

Here are some useful time-management techniques:

- **Prioritize tasks:** Make a to-do list and prioritize your tasks based on urgency and importance. Focus on completing high-priority tasks first before moving on to less important ones.
- **Set specific goals:** Set clear, achievable goals for your day, week, or month. This will give you a sense of direction and purpose, helping you stay motivated and focused.
- **Break tasks into smaller steps:** Large tasks can feel overwhelming, so break them down into smaller, more manageable steps. This will help you make progress and avoid procrastination.
- **Use a calendar or planner:** Keep track of your appointments, deadlines, and important dates using a calendar or planner. This will help you stay organized and ensure that you don't forget anything important.
- **Eliminate distractions:** Identify your biggest distractions and find ways to minimize or eliminate them. This could include turning off notifications, setting specific work hours, or working in a quiet environment.
- **Delegate tasks:** If possible, delegate tasks to others to free up your time for more important or high-

priority activities. Delegating can help you be more efficient and make better use of your resources.

- **Learn to say no:** It's important to set boundaries and learn to say no to tasks or commitments that do not align with your goals or priorities. This will help you avoid overcommitting and feeling overwhelmed.
- **Pomodoro Technique:** The Pomodoro Technique is a time management method developed by Francesco Cirillo in the late 1980s. It involves breaking your work into intervals, traditionally 25 minutes in length, separated by short breaks. Here's how it typically works:
- Choose a task you want to work on.
- Set a timer for 25 minutes (this is called a "Pomodoro").
- Work on the task until the timer rings.
- Take a short break (around 5 minutes).
- Repeat this process: after four Pomodoros, take a longer break (around 15–30 minutes).
- **Eat the Frog Technique:** This technique is based on the concept of tackling your most challenging or unpleasant task first thing in the morning; essentially, "eating the frog" means completing the task you want to procrastinate on the most. The idea is that once you've completed the hardest task, the rest of your day will feel easier and more productive. By facing the

most difficult task head-on, you can prevent it from weighing on you throughout the day and potentially delaying other tasks.

Setting Boundaries

Learning to say no and setting boundaries in your personal and professional life is essential for reducing stress. By establishing clear limits and honoring your own needs, you can prevent burnout and overwhelm.

Here's how you do it:

- **Identify your limits:** Take some time to reflect on what makes you feel uncomfortable, stressed, or unhappy in your relationships. This will help you define your boundaries more clearly.
- **Communicate assertively:** Clearly and respectfully communicate your boundaries to others. Use "I" statements to express your needs and wants. For example, "I feel overwhelmed when I am asked to work overtime every day. I need to limit my working hours."
- **Be consistent:** Once you've set your boundaries, stick to them. Consistency is key to establishing and maintaining healthy boundaries.
- **Practice self-care:** Setting boundaries also means taking care of yourself. Make time for self-care activities that nurture your physical, emotional, and mental well-being.

- **Seek support:** If you're finding it challenging to set or maintain boundaries, consider seeking support from a counselor, therapist, or trusted friend. They can provide guidance and encouragement as you navigate this process.

Remember, setting boundaries is a skill that takes practice. Be patient with yourself and trust that you deserve to have your boundaries respected.

Self-Care Practices

No, it is not selfish to focus on yourself and enjoy self-care. It's a necessity that we all need to learn to do more of.

Engaging in regular self-care activities such as reading a book, taking a bubble bath, or practicing a hobby you enjoy can help you relax and recharge. Making time for yourself is essential for maintaining a healthy balance in your life.

Incorporating these stress management techniques into your daily routine can help you build resilience and cope with stress more effectively. Remember to be patient with yourself and experiment with different strategies to find what works best for you. By taking proactive steps to manage your stress, you can improve your overall well-being and quality of life.

The Importance of Sleep and Relaxation

In today's fast-paced world, prioritizing sleep and relaxation may often take a backseat to the demands of daily life. However, the benefits of a good night's rest and regular relaxation practices cannot be overstated when it comes to maintaining overall health and well-being. From improved cognitive function to a strengthened immune system, quality sleep and relaxation are essential pillars of a healthy lifestyle.

Sleep isn't lazy or a time to do just nothing; it is a crucial physiological process that allows our bodies and minds to recharge and repair. Adequate sleep is essential for optimal physical, mental, and emotional functioning. Research has shown that a lack of sleep can have a detrimental impact on various aspects of health, including cognitive function, mood regulation, immune function, and metabolic health.

When you're sleep-deprived, nothing good comes of it. In fact, even one night of poor sleep can leave you in a sleep debt you badly need to pay back.

One of the key reasons why sleep is so important for good health is its role in cognitive function. During sleep, the brain consolidates memories, processes information, and rejuvenates neural pathways. Inadequate sleep can impair concentration, memory, and decision-making skills, ultimately hindering our ability to perform daily tasks effectively.

On top of that, sleep plays a critical role in supporting overall immune function. A well-rested body is better equipped to fight off infections and illnesses, as sleep helps regulate the immune response and promotes the production of cytokines, which are crucial in fighting off inflammation and infection.

Furthermore, sleep is closely linked to metabolic health. Chronic sleep deprivation has been associated with an increased risk of obesity, diabetes, and cardiovascular disease. Poor sleep can disrupt hormone regulation, leading to imbalances in appetite-regulating hormones such as leptin and ghrelin, which can contribute to weight gain and metabolic dysfunction.

It's not just sleep that's so important; but general relaxation too.

Incorporating relaxation practices into our daily routine is essential for managing stress and promoting overall well-being. Chronic stress can have a profound impact on our physical and mental health, contributing to a range of health issues such as high blood pressure, anxiety, depression, and insomnia.

Relaxation techniques such as deep breathing, meditation, yoga, and tai chi can help lower stress levels, reduce anxiety, and promote a sense of calm and balance. By activating the body's relaxation response, these practices can counteract the harmful effects of chronic stress, leading to improved mental clarity, emotional stability, and physical health.

Tips for Good Sleep Hygiene

Developing good sleep hygiene practices is essential for ensuring restful and restorative sleep. Here are some tips to help improve the quality of your sleep:

- **Establish a Regular Sleep Schedule:** Try to go to bed and wake up at the same time every day, even on weekends. Consistency helps regulate your body's internal clock, making it easier to fall asleep and wake up naturally.

- **Create a Relaxing Bedtime Routine:** Engage in calming activities before bed, such as reading, taking a warm bath, or practicing relaxation techniques. Avoid stimulating activities like watching TV or using electronic devices, as the blue light emitted can disrupt your body's natural sleep-wake cycle.

- **Create a Comfortable Sleep Environment:** Make sure your bedroom is cool, dark, and quiet to create an ideal sleep environment. Invest in a comfortable mattress and pillows that support a good night's rest. In fact, when was the last time you changed your pillows? Perhaps it's time.

- **Limit Caffeine and Alcohol Intake:** Avoid consuming caffeine and alcohol close to bedtime, as they can interfere with your ability to fall asleep and stay asleep.
- **Exercise Regularly:** Regular physical activity can help improve sleep quality and overall health. Aim for at least 30 minutes of moderate exercise most days of the week, but avoid vigorous exercise close to bedtime.
- **Manage Stress:** Incorporate relaxation techniques into your daily routine to help manage stress and promote relaxation. Deep breathing exercises, meditation, and mindfulness can help calm the mind and prepare the body for restful sleep.

Remember, prioritizing sleep and relaxation is essential for achieving optimal health and well-being. Quality sleep is not a luxury but a fundamental need that supports physical, mental, and emotional health. It's vital.

Exercise and its Effects on the Vagus Nerve

Exercise is a powerful tool that can have profound effects on the vagus nerve, impacting our overall well-being in ways we might not even realize. When we engage in physical activity, we are not just working our muscles and cardiovascular system; we are also influencing the intricate network of the vagus nerve and the autonomic nervous system as a whole.

One of the key ways in which exercise affects the vagus nerve is through its ability to increase heart rate variability (HRV). HRV is a measure of the variation in time intervals between heartbeats, which reflects the balance between the sympathetic and parasympathetic branches of the autonomic nervous system. The vagus nerve plays a crucial role in this balance, as it is responsible for activating the parasympathetic response that helps to calm the body and reduce stress.

Regular exercise has been shown to increase HRV, indicating a stronger parasympathetic tone and better overall autonomic nervous system function. This can lead to improved stress resilience, better emotional regulation, and enhanced recovery from physical and mental exertion. In other words, exercise can help us stay calm under pressure and bounce back more quickly from life's challenges.

Furthermore, exercise has been found to stimulate the release of neurotransmitters such as acetylcholine and norepinephrine, which play important roles in regulating the activity of the vagus nerve. These neurotransmitters can enhance the connection between the brain and the body, promoting better communication and coordination between different systems. This improved neural efficiency can result in greater physical performance, faster reaction times, and enhanced cognitive function.

So, what are some good exercises to do in order to reap these benefits for the vagus nerve? Here are a few examples:

- **Yoga:** Yoga combines physical postures, breathwork, and mindfulness practices that can help stimulate the vagus nerve and promote relaxation. Poses such as Child's Pose, Bridge Pose, and Legs-Up-the-Wall are particularly effective for activating the parasympathetic response.

- **Cardiovascular exercise:** Activities such as running, cycling, swimming, and dancing can elevate heart rate variability and improve overall autonomic function. Aim for moderate-intensity exercise for at least 30 minutes most days of the week.

- **Strength training:** Resistance training not only builds muscle strength but also enhances neural connections and coordination. Exercises like squats, deadlifts, push-ups, and rows can engage the vagus nerve and improve overall nervous system health.

- **Mind-body practices:** Activities like tai chi, qigong, and Pilates combine movement with mindfulness and breath awareness, creating a holistic approach to improving vagal tone and overall well-being.

The recommended amount of exercise per week for adults is at least 150 minutes of moderate-intensity aerobic activity, such as brisk walking or cycling, or 75 minutes of vigorous-intensity aerobic activity, such as running or swimming. It's also beneficial to include muscle-strengthening activities on two or more days per week. Remember, it's important to find activities you enjoy to make exercise a sustainable and enjoyable part of your lifestyle.

Incorporating a variety of exercises into your routine can help to keep the vagus nerve healthy and functioning optimally. Remember to listen to your body, pay attention to how you feel during and after exercise, and adjust your routine as needed to support your overall health and well-being. So, lace up those running shoes, roll out your yoga mat, or grab those dumbbells - your vagus nerve will thank you!

Chapter 11

Case Studies and Personal Stories

It's all very well and good reading about why the vagus nerve is important and how stimulating it leads to overall health and well-being. But you want to hear and see results, right? That means you want to hear some real-life stories of people who made it work for them.

So, before we move on to our last chapter, let's quickly give you exactly what you want.

Case Study 1: Sarah's Journey to Inner Harmony

Meet Sarah, a vibrant soul who had long struggled with anxiety and digestive issues. After extensive research, she embarked on a journey to improve her vagal tone through a combination of yoga, deep breathing exercises, and cold water immersion.

By regularly engaging in these practices, Sarah noticed a significant reduction in her anxiety levels and a remarkable improvement in her digestion. She describes the sensation of calm washing over her, like a soothing wave emanating from deep within.

Through her journey, Sarah learned the invaluable lesson that true healing begins from within, and that by nurturing her vagus nerve, she could cultivate a profound sense of inner harmony.

Case Study 2: David's Resilience Revolution

David, a former elite athlete, faced a challenging transition into retirement, grappling with feelings of purposelessness and depression. Determined to reclaim his vitality, he delved into the world of vagus nerve stimulation, exploring techniques such as sound therapy, meditation, and heart rate variability training.

Through consistent practice, David experienced a remarkable shift in his emotional well-being, finding newfound resilience and a sense of purpose in life. He describes the sensation of his heart rhythm aligning with the rhythm of the universe, a powerful reminder of the interconnectedness of all living beings.

For David, the journey of enhancing his vagal tone became a transformative revolution, empowering him to navigate life's ups and downs with grace and strength.

Case Study 3: Maria's Metamorphosis Through Breathwork

Maria, a busy professional juggling multiple responsibilities, found herself constantly battling stress and fatigue. Seeking a holistic approach to wellness, she delved into the practice of breathwork, a powerful tool for stimulating the vagus nerve and promoting relaxation.

Through rhythmic breathing exercises and guided meditation, Maria discovered a profound sense of mental clarity and rejuvenation. She describes the sensation of her breath becoming a conduit for inner peace, harmonizing her mind and body in a symphony of healing.

Through her journey, Maria learned the profound impact of conscious breathing on her overall well-being, awakening to the transformative potential of the mind-body connection.

Case Study 4: Mark's Mindful Mastery of Stress

Mark, a high-powered executive navigating the pressures of corporate life, found himself plagued by chronic stress and burnout. Seeking a sustainable solution to his mental health struggles, he delved into the practice of mindfulness, gradually honing his ability to cultivate present-moment awareness and inner calm.

Through mindfulness meditation, somatic experiencing, and Qi Gong practices, Mark experienced a profound shift in his stress response, learning to navigate life's challenges with equanimity and resilience. He describes the sensation of his body becoming a sanctuary of stillness, a refuge from the chaos of the external world.

For Mark, the journey of mastering his mind through vagus nerve stimulation became a powerful lesson in the art of self-care and self-mastery.

Case Study 5: Sarah and David's Sacred Connection

Sarah and David, two kindred spirits united by their shared passion for holistic healing, embarked on a transformative journey together, exploring the depths of vagus nerve stimulation and its profound impact on their lives.

Through a fusion of practices such as partner yoga, heartfelt conversations, and therapeutic touch, Sarah and David cultivated a deep sense of connection and empathy, nourishing their vagal wellness and strengthening their bond. They describe the sensation of their energies intertwining, creating a sacred space of healing and love that radiated outwards, uplifting those around them.

For Sarah and David, the journey of shared vagal exploration became a testament to the transformative power of human connection and the ripple effect of wellness in fostering a more compassionate world.

Case Studies and Personal Stories

Through the power of holistic practices, conscious awareness, and a deep commitment to self-care, these people unlocked a treasure trove of healing potential within themselves, paving the way for a life of profound well-being and vitality. May their stories serve as a beacon of hope and inspiration for all who seek to embark on their own journey of vagal exploration, reminding us that the path to true healing begins by listening to the whispers of our own wandering nerves.

Chapter 12

Future Directions and Conclusion

As we reach the end of our journey into the vagus nerve, let's look to the future.

What might we be able to use vagal nerve stimulation for as the years tick by? What areas do researchers see promise in?

Let's delve deeper.

While traditionally associated with regulating essential bodily functions like heart rate and digestion, recent research has uncovered a wealth of potential applications for vagal nerve stimulation (VNS) that extend far beyond its original scope.

As we delve into the realm of emerging research, it becomes increasingly evident that the vagus nerve holds the key to unlocking a myriad of therapeutic possibilities. Let's explore some of the cutting-edge studies and potential future uses of VNS that are shaping the landscape of modern medicine.

Mood Disorders and Depression

One of the most promising areas of research involving VNS is its potential to treat mood disorders such as depression. Studies have shown that stimulating the vagus nerve can have a profound effect on mood regulation by influencing the release of neurotransmitters like serotonin and norepinephrine.

This has led to the development of VNS as a therapy for treatment-resistant depression, offering hope for those who have not responded to traditional antidepressant medications.

In the future, we may see VNS used more widely as a non-invasive and effective treatment for various mood disorders, providing patients with a new avenue for managing their mental health.

Chronic Pain Management

Chronic pain is a complex condition that can significantly impact a person's quality of life. VNS has emerged as a promising alternative for managing chronic pain by modulating pain perception pathways in the brain.

Research suggests that stimulating the vagus nerve can reduce the intensity of pain signals and provide long-lasting relief for individuals suffering from conditions such as fibromyalgia, neuropathic pain, and migraines.

With further advancements in VNS technology and research, we can anticipate more personalized and targeted approaches to managing chronic pain, offering patients a safe and effective alternative to traditional pain management strategies.

Inflammatory Disorders

Inflammation is a common denominator in a wide range of health conditions, from autoimmune diseases to metabolic disorders. VNS has shown great potential for modulating the body's inflammatory response by inhibiting the release of pro-inflammatory cytokines and promoting anti-inflammatory pathways.

This has sparked interest in using VNS as a therapy for conditions like rheumatoid arthritis, inflammatory bowel disease, and even metabolic syndrome.

As researchers continue to unravel the intricate mechanisms behind VNS's anti-inflammatory effects, we may witness the development of novel therapies that target inflammation at its core, offering new hope for patients grappling with chronic inflammatory disorders.

Cognitive Enhancement and Memory

The idea of enhancing cognitive function and memory through VNS may seem like something out of a science fiction novel, but recent research has shown that stimulating the vagus nerve can indeed have profound effects on cognitive processing and memory consolidation.

By improving communication between different brain regions and enhancing neuroplasticity, VNS holds promise as a potential therapy for enhancing cognitive performance in both healthy individuals and those with cognitive impairments.

In the future, we could see VNS being explored as a tool for enhancing memory retention, boosting learning capabilities, and even slowing down cognitive decline in conditions like Alzheimer's disease.

Cardiovascular Health

Given the vagus nerve's integral role in regulating heart rate and cardiovascular function, it comes as no surprise that VNS has been investigated as a potential therapy for enhancing cardiovascular health. By modulating the autonomic nervous system, VNS can help regulate blood pressure, heart rate variability, and overall cardiac function, making it a promising adjunctive treatment for conditions like hypertension, heart failure, and arrhythmias.

As researchers delve deeper into the cardiovascular benefits of VNS, we may witness the emergence of innovative therapies that target specific aspects of cardiovascular health, offering patients a holistic approach to managing their heart health.

Future Directions and Conclusion

In conclusion, the future of vagal nerve stimulation is brimming with possibilities, each holding the potential to transform the landscape of modern medicine. From treating mood disorders and chronic pain to managing inflammatory conditions and enhancing cognitive function, VNS offers a versatile and promising platform for addressing a wide array of health challenges.

As researchers continue to push the boundaries of knowledge and innovation, we can look forward to a future where vagal nerve stimulation plays a prominent role in revolutionizing healthcare and improving the lives of countless individuals worldwide. The journey towards unlocking the full potential of VNS may be ongoing, but with each new discovery and breakthrough, we move one step closer to a future where the healing power of the vagus nerve knows no bounds.

Resources for Further Learning

Understanding the functions and potential benefits of optimizing vagal tone has become an area of growing interest in the wellness and medical communities. If you're looking to delve deeper into the world of the vagus nerve, there are numerous resources available to expand knowledge, find support, and connect with like-minded individuals.

Books on the Vagus Nerve

One of the best ways to deepen your understanding of the vagus nerve is through books written by experts in the field. Several notable books provide valuable insights into the science behind the vagus nerve, as well as practical tips for harnessing its power.

- **"The Polyvagal Theory: Neurophysiological Foundations of Emotions, Attachment, Communication, and Self-Regulation" by Stephen Porges:** This seminal work explores the polyvagal theory, a groundbreaking concept that illuminates the role of the vagus nerve in our emotional and social lives.

- **"Accessing the Healing Power of the Vagus Nerve: Self-Help Exercises for Anxiety, Depression, Trauma, and Autism" by Stanley Rosenberg:** In this practical guide, Rosenberg offers a wealth of exercises and techniques for improving vagal tone and promoting overall well-being.

- **"The Body Keeps the Score: Brain, Mind, and Body in the Healing of Trauma" by Bessel van der Kolk:** While not solely focused on the vagus nerve, this book delves into the profound impact of trauma on the body and mind, emphasizing the role of the vagus nerve in the healing process.

Online Resources

The internet is a treasure trove of information on the vagus nerve, with numerous websites, podcasts, and online communities dedicated to exploring its intricacies. Here are some online resources that can help you further your learning journey:

- **Vagus Nerve Hub (vagusnervehub.com):** This comprehensive website offers articles, interviews, and resources on the vagus nerve, covering topics such as vagal tone, vagus nerve stimulation, and polyvagal theory.

- **"The Vagus Nerve: An Owner's Manual" Podcast:** Hosted by a team of experts in psychology and neuroscience, this podcast delves into the fascinating world of the vagus nerve, offering insights and practical tips for enhancing vagal tone.
- **Social Media Groups:** Platforms such as Facebook and Reddit host communities of individuals interested in the vagus nerve and related topics. Joining these groups can provide opportunities to connect with like-minded individuals, share experiences, and learn from others' perspectives.

Workshops and Courses

For those seeking a more hands-on approach to learning about the vagus nerve, attending workshops or enrolling in courses can offer valuable opportunities for in-depth exploration.

Many wellness centers, yoga studios, and health clinics offer workshops focused on vagal health and regulation. Additionally, several online platforms host courses taught by experts in the field. Here are a few options to consider:

- **The Vagus Nerve Workshop at The Breathing Project:** This workshop offers practical exercises and techniques for activating and toning the vagus nerve through breathwork, movement, and mindfulness practices.

- **"Healing Trauma: A Brief Mindful Pause" Course on Insight Timer:** Led by a trauma-informed mindfulness teacher, this course explores the connection between trauma, the nervous system, and the vagus nerve, offering practices for healing and regulation.
- **Online Vagus Nerve Retreats:** Some wellness retreat centers offer virtual retreats focused on vagal health and well-being. These retreats typically include workshops, guided meditations, and discussions led by experts in the field.

Medical Professionals and Therapists

If you're looking for personalized guidance and support in exploring the vagus nerve, seeking out medical professionals and therapists with expertise in this area can be beneficial.

Integrative medicine practitioners, functional medicine doctors, and therapists specializing in trauma-informed care may offer insights and techniques for enhancing vagal tone and overall well-being.

Conclusion

Congratulations! You've reached the end of this book and clearly demonstrated your keenness to learn more about the vagus nerve and harness its tremendous potential.

In conclusion, the vagus nerve is a fascinating and powerful pathway in our bodies that connects our brain to almost every organ. Throughout this book, we've delved into the intricate functions of the vagus nerve, understanding how it influences our emotional well-being, immune response, digestion, heart health, and more. We've explored the ways in which vagal tone can be enhanced through various stimulation techniques, leading to improved overall health and well-being.

As we wrap up our journey through the wonders of the vagus nerve, it's important to acknowledge the incredible potential that lies within each of us to optimize our vagal tone. By incorporating simple yet effective practices such as deep breathing exercises, meditation, yoga, mindfulness, social connections, laughter, cold exposure, and physical activity into our daily routines, we can actively stimulate and strengthen our vagus nerve.

Imagine a life where stress and anxiety no longer hold you captive, where your immune system is robust and resilient, where your digestion is smooth and efficient, and where your heart beats in harmony with your emotions. This is the reality that awaits those who choose to prioritize their vagal tone and take proactive steps towards enhancing it.

So, dear reader, I encourage you to embark on this journey of self-discovery and empowerment. Start by incorporating one simple vagal stimulation technique into your daily routine today. Whether it's practicing a few minutes of deep belly breathing in the morning, engaging in a heartwarming conversation with a loved one, or immersing yourself in the healing power of nature, every small step you take towards improving your vagal tone matters.

And remember, progress is not about perfection. It's about consistency and commitment to your own well-being. Be gentle with yourself, celebrate your victories no matter how small, and trust in the wisdom of your body to guide you towards greater health and vitality.

As you continue on your journey towards better vagal tone and overall wellness, I leave you with this empowering thought: you have the power to influence the health of your vagus nerve and, in doing so, transform your life for the better. Embrace the potential that lies within you, nurture your vagus nerve with care and intention, and watch as a newfound sense of balance, resilience, and joy blossoms within you.

May your journey be filled with moments of healing, growth, and transformation. May your vagus nerve be a beacon of light, guiding you toward a life of vitality and well-being. May you always remember that the power to heal is within you.

References

Bolster your brain by stimulating the vagus nerve. (n.d.). Cedars-Sinai. https://www.cedars-sinai.org/blog/stimulating-the-vagus-nerve.html

Burton, N. (2022, November 7). *4 Meditations to stimulate the vagus nerve.* DailyOM.com. https://www.dailyom.com/journal/meditations-to-stimulate-the-vagus-nerve/

Clinic, C. (2024, June 27). *5 ways to stimulate your vagus nerve.* Cleveland Clinic. https://health.clevelandclinic.org/vagus-nerve-stimulation

Gonzalez, A. (2024, May 2). *A 12-Minute breathing practice to activate your vagus nerve.* Mindful. https://www.mindful.org/a-12-minute-breathing-practice-to-activate-your-vagus-nerve/

Hersh, E. (2024, March 27). *12 healthy sleep hygiene tips.* Healthline. https://www.healthline.com/health/sleep-hygiene

Hoehl, S., & Bertenthal, B. I. (2021). An interactionist perspective on the development of coordinated social attention. *Advances in Child Development and Behavior*, 1–41. https://doi.org/10.1016/bs.acdb.2021.05.001

Kate. (2024, May 10). *6 Vagus nerve Exercises to boost your Well-being – free online yoga video.* YogaUOnline. https://yogauonline.com/yoga-practice-teaching-tips/yoga-practice-tips/6-ways-to-stimulate-your-vagus-nerve-with-yoga-and-breathing/

Kenny, B. J., & Bordoni, B. (2022, November 7). *Neuroanatomy, cranial nerve 10 (Vagus nerve).* StatPearls - NCBI Bookshelf. https://www.ncbi.nlm.nih.gov/books/NBK537171/

Neff, M. A. (2023, September 8). *Improve vagal tone.* Insights of a Neurodivergent Clinician. https://neurodivergentinsights.com/blog/how-to-improve-vagal-tone

Practicing deep breathing for better physical and mental health. | OneStep Digital Physical Therapy. (n.d.). https://www.onestep.co/resources-blog/deep-breathing-better-physical-mental-health#:~:text=The%20relationship%20between%20breathing%20and,of%20stress%20hormones%20like%20cortisol.

Professional, C. C. M. (n.d.). *Vagus nerve.* Cleveland Clinic. https://my.clevelandclinic.org/health/body/22279-vagus-nerve

Robinson, L., & Smith, M., MA. (2024, May 14). Stress Management: Techniques & Strategies to Deal with Stress. *HelpGuide.org.* https://www.helpguide.org/articles/stress/stress-management.htm

Ruscio, M., DC, & Ruscio, M., DC. (2024, May 9). *What is vagal tone and how to improve yours - Dr. Michael Ruscio, DC.* Dr. Michael Ruscio, DC. https://drruscio.com/vagal-tone/

References

Segal, D. (2022, October 6). *Vagus nerve: What to know*. WebMD. https://www.webmd.com/brain/vagus-nerve-what-to-know

Seladi-Schulman, J., PhD. (2023, February 14). *What is the Vagus Nerve?* Healthline. https://www.healthline.com/human-body-maps/vagus-nerve

Stress management - Mayo Clinic. (2023, October 26). https://www.mayoclinic.org/tests-procedures/stress-management/about/pac-20384898#:~:text=Stress%20management%20approaches%20include%3A,your%20emotional%20awareness%20and%20reactions.

Suni, E., & Suni, E. (2024, March 4). *Mastering Sleep Hygiene: Your path to quality sleep*. Sleep Foundation. https://www.sleepfoundation.org/sleep-hygiene

The Editors of Encyclopaedia Britannica. (2024, June 20). *Vagus nerve | Definition, Function, & Facts*. Encyclopedia Britannica. https://www.britannica.com/science/vagus-nerve

Vagal tone: a physiologic marker of stress vulnerability. (1992, September 1). PubMed. https://pubmed.ncbi.nlm.nih.gov/1513615/

Wikipedia contributors. (2024a, July 1). *Vagus nerve*. Wikipedia. https://en.wikipedia.org/wiki/Vagus_nerve

Wikipedia contributors. (2024b, July 13). *Vagal tone*. Wikipedia. https://en.wikipedia.org/wiki/Vagal_tone#:~:text=Vagal%20tone%20is%20activity%20of,several%20body%20compartments%20at%20rest.

Printed in Great Britain
by Amazon